Battles of the '45

BATTLES OF THE '45

KATHERINE TOMASSON
&
FRANCIS BUIST

LONDON
B. T. BATSFORD LTD

First published 1962
Reprinted 1978

MADE AND PRINTED IN GREAT BRITAIN BY
REDWOOD BURN LIMITED, TROWBRIDGE AND ESHER

FOREWORD

As this is not a full-length history of the Forty-five, the narrative of events leading up to the three principal actions is intended to do no more than set the stage for them. In consequence, some incidents, such as the skirmish at Inverurie, have been omitted.

In describing the battles certain sources of information were found particularly valuable. Those dealing with Prestonpans were the report of Sir John Cope's 'Examination', and Sir Robert Cadell's defence of that much-ridiculed general. Similarly, a statement written by the unfortunate Captain Cuningham, among the Cumberland Papers, contained interesting details concerning the artillery train at Falkirk.

The *Memoirs* of Sir John MacDonald, written in French, and included in Henrietta Tayler's *Jacobite Miscellany*, provided an important clue, by means of which the foundation stones of the south and east walls of the old Culloden enclosures could be identified. It was thus possible to establish the original length and position of the Jacobite front line; similarly, a slight rise to the east of what then seems to have been marshy ground showed where Cumberland's right wing was probably drawn up. The positions of the regiments of both armies shown in the plan are based on these observations.

It should be noted that the numbers of certain British regiments mentioned in the narrative—Lee's (55th), Murray's (57th), Lascelles's (58th), and Ligonier's (59th)—are those they bore in 1745. Later, following the Peace of Aix-la-Chapelle (1748) and the reduction of several regiments, including Battereau's and Lord Loudon's Highlanders, these four became, respectively, the 44th, 46th, 47th, and 48th.

Finally, in the account of Culloden, Bligh's, Munro's, and Ligonier's regiments have been so designated to avoid confusion; in fact, new commanding officers had been appointed to all three shortly before the battle.

CONTENTS

ACKNOWLEDGMENT

Extracts from the Cumberland Papers are printed by the gracious permission of Her Majesty The Queen.

Those from an unpublished letter and notes of Lord George Murray are included by kind permission of His Grace the Duke of Atholl, and quotations from items in the Blaikie Collection by courtesy of the Trustees of the National Library of Scotland. The courtesy of the Trustees of the unpublished Newcastle MSS is similarly acknowledged in permitting quotations from the letter of Lord Mark Kerr.

The authors are grateful to many people for their assistance, and would mention in particular Mr. Norman Crawford, formerly Librarian and Curator, Arbroath Public Library; the late Mr. P. E. T. Edwards of the Department of Manuscripts, British Museum; the late Mr. C. I. Fraser, Reelig House, Kirkhill, Inverness-shire; Mr. A. N. Kennard, F.S.A., formerly of The Armouries, H.M. Tower of London; the staffs of the National Library of Scotland, and of the Scottish Record Office; the Secretary of the Royal Artillery Institution, Woolwich; Mr. W. A. Thorburn, Keeper of the Scottish United Services Museum, Edinburgh Castle; Miss E. L. Watson, formerly of the Reference Department, Sandeman Public Library, Perth; and Sir Robin Mackworth-Young, K.C.V.O., F.S.A., Librarian, Windsor Castle.

For the illustrations, acknowledgment is due to:

Her Majesty The Queen, for no. 28
The Duke of Atholl, for nos 3, 8, 20
The Earl of Ancaster, for no. 15
The Trustees of the British Museum, for nos 9, 10, 17, 21, 22, 23, 24, 25, 29, 30, 33
The Marquess of Bute, for no. 4
The Lancaster Museum, for nos 31, 34
The Marquess of Lothian, for no. 19

9

ACKNOWLEDGMENT

The MacBean Collection, University Library, King's College, Aberdeen, for no. 1
The National Galleries of Scotland, for nos 2, 5, 13, 16, 27, 32
The National Portrait Gallery, for no. 14
Sir David Ogilvy, for no. 11
The Parker Gallery, for no. 26
The Earl of Perth, for no. 7
Radio Times Hulton Picture Library, for no. 6
Royal Albert Memorial Museum, Exeter, for no. 18
Captain Michael Wemyss, for no. 12

LIST OF ILLUSTRATIONS

LIST OF ILLUSTRATIONS

LIST OF ILLUSTRATIONS

I

The Jacobite Background

ON 5TH SEPTEMBER 1701, 13 years after his abdication, King James the Second died in exile at St. Germain. His fight to regain his throne had ended in failure, but during the next 44 years no fewer than five attempts were to be made to bring 'the auld Stuarts back again'.

The year after James's death his younger daughter, Anne, became Queen in succession to her brother-in-law, William of Orange, but this event gave little satisfaction to the late King's supporters. She was, it was true, a Stuart, but unless—which seemed unlikely—she could produce an heir to succeed her, she would be destined to become the last of her line, for the Crown would then pass to the Protestant Electress Sophia of Hanover and her successors, to the exclusion of Anne's half-brother, James.

James's birth, in 1688, had been the final cause of his father's undoing. Whig propaganda alleged that he had been smuggled into the Queen's bed in a warming pan, but in appearance and temperament he bore an unmistakable resemblance to his parents. Nicknamed 'The Blackbird', he had the dark eyes and swarthy complexion of his Italian mother, and his father's uncompromising respect for principle. His firm refusal to abandon Roman Catholicism for the sake of political expediency was to prove a serious handicap to his followers.

Almost as great a handicap was the Jacobites' reliance on foreign assistance. As the wealthiest and most populous of the three Kingdoms it was upon England that any hope of a Stuart restoration finally depended, and to the majority of Englishmen such intervention was a gross interference in the nation's domestic affairs. If a change of dynasty were necessary, it should be brought about by the people of England, not by foreigners like the French, who in addition to being inveterate enemies were James's co-religionists. The Scots were hardly less suspect, for although the crowns of England and Scotland had been united for almost a hundred years, and the two countries were shortly to be still more closely linked, the long-standing enmity between them was to smoulder on.

To the French, the Jacobites were a useful, but unreliable, fifth-column, and in giving them military support French interests rather than James's were the primary consideration. Any side-show mounted on their behalf was expected to pay its way, usually by diverting British troops from the main theatre of war, and on at least one occasion this policy was remarkably successful. Nevertheless, in staging these diversions the French took considerable risks, for 'security' was as yet unknown, and the Royal Navy invariably had ample notice of their intentions. They had also to face the danger of storm-damage, as the Spaniards were to discover when attempting to carry out a similar operation in 1719.

In promoting the claims of the young prince and a second Restoration the Jacobites were ready to exploit any favourable opportunity, and in Scotland the widespread opposition to the Act of Union (1707) provided them with an excellent opening. Following what was to become the familiar blue-print of later attempts, it was planned to raise an insurrection to coincide with the arrival of a French expeditionary force, and in March 1708 6,000 French troops set sail from Dunkirk, escorted by five battleships under the command of Count de Forbin. Aboard his flagship was the 19-year-old claimant, and de Forbin's orders were to put him ashore with the troops on the south shore of the Firth of Forth, where on being joined by his Scottish supporters he would march directly on Edinburgh.

With his usual ill-luck James fell sick on the eve of sailing, and the delay gave an inquisitive British squadron plenty of time to observe the French preparations. A further delay was caused by the French fleet overshooting its mark, but it eventually reached the Firth of Forth on the evening of 12th March, and during the night unsuccessful attempts were made to communicate with the Jacobite leaders ashore. Next morning the reason for their failure became evident, for when daylight dawned it disclosed a strong British squadron under Sir George Byng at anchor between de Forbin and the open sea.

On sighting each other both sides got under way, and de Forbin sailed up boldly as if to attack, but while the British ships were forming line of battle he suddenly altered course, and ordering his fleet to crowd on all sail succeeded in getting clear of the mouth of the Firth. On his advice the troops had been embarked in swift-sailing privateers instead of the usual lumbering transports, and although Byng gave chase, de Forbin returned to Dunkirk with the loss of a single man-of-war and half a dozen troop carriers.

Although almost forgotten, this French expedition was destined to be the largest ever to come within striking distance of the shores of Britain in support of James.

The death of Queen Anne in 1714 found the Jacobites entirely unprepared, but although the accession of George I was carried through by their opponents with little difficulty, they soon made it clear that the 'wee, wee German lairdie' was not to enjoy undisputed possession of his new 'kailyard'. To the Government the outbreak of the 'Fifteen was no bolt from the blue, and having received warning that a French invasion was being planned in conjunction with Jacobite insurrections in England and Scotland, precautions were taken to deal with the emergency. As a result of these England remained quiet, but Scotland was again the storm-centre, and on 6th September John, 6th Earl of Mar, raised King James's standard at Braemar.

A political adventurer, whose guiding principle was self-interest, Mar was not nicknamed 'Bobbing John' for nothing. It was in keeping with his character that when the new King was on his way to England Mar had written to assure him of his undying loyalty, and had George I retained him in office it is unlikely that the 'Fifteen would have taken place. In contrast to Mar, who had next to no military experience, his opponent was a man of first-rate ability, for apart from his powerful influence as head of the great Clan Campbell, John, 2nd Duke of Argyll, had a high reputation as a statesman, and as a general was ranked second only to Marlborough.

Having made his way slowly southwards to Perth, Mar was quickly joined by reinforcements not only from the Highlands but from the counties of Perth, Angus, and Fife, so that by the beginning of October his army numbered over 6,500 men. Argyll, on the other hand, had fewer than 2,000 regular troops under his command, and these he hastily assembled at Stirling, where they were joined by 600 volunteers from Glasgow. It was a critical moment, and if Mar had had the courage to continue his southward advance, Argyll could have done little to stop him. Instead, as one of his officers sarcastically remarked, he 'did nothing all this while but write'.

Even at this early stage Mar may well have begun to have misgivings. The death of Louis XIV a few days before the outbreak of the Rising had brought about a change in policy that put an end to any hopes of large-scale French intervention. As for the much-vaunted English insurrection, it had so far amounted to no more than a handful of north-country squires and their retainers. This pathetic little band, after wandering aimlessly about the Border, finally succeeded in linking up with a few hundred Lowland Jacobites under Lords Kenmure and Nithsdale; meanwhile, although knowing nothing of their whereabouts or plans, Mar sent off a detachment to their assistance.

This force of over 1,000 men consisted largely of Highlanders, and having crossed the Forth in fishing boats its commander, Mackintosh of Borlum, conceived the bold plan of attacking Edinburgh. Argyll, however, had got wind of it, and on his sudden arrival there with 500 dragoons and mounted infantry from Stirling, Mackintosh sheered off to Leith, where he and his men barricaded themselves in the old fort. The following night he slipped quietly away across Leith sands, and eventually joined forces with Kenmure at Kelso. Three weeks later, having marched into Lancashire in search of recruits, their little army surrendered at Preston on the same day as the battle of Sheriffmuir.

While Argyll was at Edinburgh dealing with Mackintosh, Mar and the rest of his army marched south towards Stirling, his cavalry pushing on as far as Dunblane. Whether this movement was merely a feint with the object of relieving pressure on Mackintosh, or a genuine attempt to force the passage of the Forth, is uncertain. Except for bringing Argyll hurrying back to Stirling it achieved nothing, and within two days Mar had returned to Perth. It was now obvious that unless he took some decisive action his army would begin to break up, and realising that his only chance of success was to make for England in the hope of gaining support, Mar set out from Perth a second time on 10th November.

Argyll had an excellent intelligence service, and that same day he called in all his available troops from Glasgow, Kilsyth, and Falkirk.

In spite of reinforcements his army numbered only 3,100 men, but he had no intention of remaining on the defensive, and on the 12th he advanced to Dunblane, while late that evening the Jacobite army reached Kinbuck, two miles farther north.

Next day, the 13th, was fought the battle of Sheriffmuir, a scrambling, untidy affair, in which Argyll's right wing drove Mar's left across the Allan Water, while on the left the Duke's army was defeated and fled back to Stirling. Despite the words of the old song: 'There's some say that we wan, some say that they wan', the honours rested with Argyll, for from the Jacobite point of view the story of the 'Fifteen after Sheriffmuir is one of anticlimax. Both armies returned to their respective bases, and although the Rising lingered on for a further two and a half months, the Cause 'was not onlie desperate but sunk'. Even the belated arrival of King James could do nothing to revive it, although it is only fair to add that soon after landing at Peterhead he had been attacked by 'three Fits of an Ague', and was far from well.

By the end of January Argyll's army had been reinforced to three times its former strength, and the Duke began to advance north-wards through deep snow. On the 31st the Jacobite army evacuated Perth, and as he crossed the frozen Tay, James made one of his few recorded *mots*: 'See, my Lord,' he remarked to Mar, 'how you have led me on to the ice.' It was now only a matter of *sauve-qui-peut*, and four days later James and Mar embarked at Montrose for France, while their army retreated by way of Aberdeen to Badenoch, where it dispersed. In the dismal aftermath of executions and attainders it was the English and Lowland Jacobites who suffered most. The clan chiefs and their followers escaped comparatively lightly, and it is possible that had they been treated less leniently Culloden might never have been fought.

Nothing about the Jacobites is more striking than the persistence with which they pursued their aims, and little more than two years after the failure of the 'Fifteen they had begun to solicit the help of Spain and Sweden. The death of Charles XII put an end to the Swedish negotiations, but to Cardinal Alberoni, the Spanish minister, the Jacobites' proposals offered a satisfactory means of avenging the recent British defeat of the Spanish fleet off Cape Passaro. They followed the familiar pattern of simultaneous insurrections in England and Scotland, supported by landings of Spanish troops and arms.

The larger of the expeditionary forces, consisting of 5,000 men commanded by James Butler, Duke of Ormonde, sailed from Cadiz for England early in March 1719; the smaller under George Keith, the Earl Marischal, left Passajes, near San Sebastian, a day later. Embarked in two frigates, Marischal's little force of 300 men reached Stornoway without incident, and on arrival there he was met by Lord Tullibardine and the Earl of Seaforth, the chief of the Mackenzies, whose clan had been chosen as the mainstay of the rising in the Highlands. With them came instructions from the Jacobite Court, and much to Marischal's chagrin these included a commission appointing Tullibardine Commander-in-Chief of the Jacobite forces in Scotland.

Having arrived at an uneasy compromise whereby Tullibardine assumed command of the troops, and the Spanish ships remained under Marischal's orders, the next question was what was to be done. Nothing had been heard of Ormonde, and long arguments followed as to whether to begin operations at once, or await his landing in England. Seaforth, in particular, was much averse to hazarding his men without additional armed support, while Marischal was in favour of immediate action. Finally it was agreed to sail for the Scottish mainland, and on 13th April the two frigates anchored in Loch Alsh. There the Spanish troops, arms, and ammunition were landed, and to make certain that there would be no second thoughts, Marischal ordered the ships to return home.

A few days later the depressing news arrived that Ormonde's fleet had been dispersed by a storm and driven back to port, and hard on the heels of this disappointment three British warships sailed up the loch and bombarded the old castle of Eilean Donan, which the Jacobites had converted into a magazine. The castle was garrisoned by 40 Spaniards, but on being attacked by landing-parties from the ships, they at once surrendered without the loss of a man.

So far there had been little response from the neighbouring clans to Tullibardine's appeals for assistance, but a false rumour that Ormonde's expedition had been refitted and was again on its way to England brought in upwards of 1,000 men. None of them, according to Marischal's brother, James Keith, was 'very fond of the enterprize', and they had some cause for their uneasiness, for disagreement between Marischal and Tullibardine had become so acute that they occupied separate camps three miles apart.

It was now reported that Major-General Wightman was on his way from Inverness with a force of Government troops, and sinking their differences, Tullibardine and Marischal decided to take up a strong defensive position on the line of his advance down Glenshiel. By so doing they hoped to be able to delay his progress until they had received further reinforcements.

The two armies met on the evening of 10th June. Both numbered about 1,100 men, but although strongly posted astride the river Shiel there was little co-ordination between the Jacobite wings and centre, and Wightman was able to deal with them in detail, making good use of four small mortars in dislodging any pockets of resistance. By the end of the summer's evening the Highlanders were in flight, and next day the Spanish troops laid down their arms. A quarter of a century was to elapse before the next Jacobite attempt was made.

Following the 'Fifteen a number of measures had been taken by the Government to establish law and order in the Highlands and reduce the chances of further outbreaks. Barracks had been built at Kilcumein (later Fort Augustus), Bernera (Glenelg), Ruthven (Badenoch), and at Inversnaid, on Loch Lomond. An act by which the Highlanders were obliged to surrender their arms had also been passed, but this had proved ineffective, and in 1724 Major-General George Wade was ordered to prepare a report on the state of the Highlands, and so to lead to their final pacification. The following year he was appointed Commander-in-Chief in Scotland, and under his supervision forts were erected at Kilcumein (Fort Augustus) and Inverness (Fort George), which, with the existing Fort William, formed what was known as 'The Chain', extending along the line of the present Caledonian Canal. To provide communication between these forts and barracks and the Lowlands, some 250 miles of roads and 40 bridges were constructed by military labour between 1725 and 1737. To deal with the arms question an Act 'for more effectual disarming the Highlands' was passed in 1725, but this was to prove as ineffectual as its predecessor, and left the loyal clans, which dutifully surrendered their arms, at the mercy of their disaffected neighbours. A more practical measure was the re-establishment of 'independent companies' of Highlanders to assist the regular troops in carrying out their duties. Such companies had been in existence since the reign of Charles II, but had latterly had to be disbanded on account of corruption. Under Wade's stricter supervision the new companies did their work well, and in due time became the nucleus of the first Highland regiment in the British Army, better known as The Black Watch.

Meanwhile in Jacobite circles the shadowy personality of King James receded into the background, to be replaced by the romantic figure of his elder son, Charles Edward. Born in 1720, the young Prince had inherited a spirit and decision from his Polish mother, Clementina Sobieska, that were in strong contrast to his father's reserved and indeterminate character. At the age of 13 he had been present at the siege of Gaeta, where to the alarm of his bear-leaders he had insisted in visiting the most exposed positions, and thenceforward it had become his ambition to attain military glory. With this end in view much of his time was spent in keeping physically fit by riding and walking, and with his tall, well-built figure and abundance of energy he seemed, in the words of an admirer, 'made for war'. Mentally, Charles was less well equipped. He was what would nowadays be called the child of a broken marriage, and his education and upbringing were unsystematic and haphazard. In spite of his taste for soldiering he never seems to have studied military subjects, and his spelling was even wilder than that of most of his contemporaries. Brought up among the petty jealousies and intrigues of the Jacobite Court, he had little knowledge of the outside world and remained in many ways a grown-up child, and in choosing the fond but foolish Sir Thomas Sheridan as his tutor King James unwittingly did his best to ruin the Prince's character.

In 1739 the long peace came to an end, when, much against Walpole's will, Britain declared war on Spain. Three years later she was drawn into conflict with France, and Jacobite hopes rose high when in the autumn of 1743 the French Government drew up plans for a large-scale attack on Britain, which was to be mounted early the following year. Although on the same lines as previous attempts the scheme was the most ambitious the French and their Jacobite allies had yet undertaken. Commanded by the Earl Marischal, 3,000 French troops were to be landed in the Highlands, where they were to be joined by the Jacobite clans, while a larger force of 12,000 men under the famous Marshal Saxe and Prince Charles Edward was to be put ashore within easy marching distance of London.

Leaving Rome incognito in January 1744, the Prince travelled to

Paris, where he discussed the plans of the expedition before going on to Gravelines to await the embarkation of the French troops at Dunkirk. By the end of February all was ready, and protected by an escorting squadron of warships from Brest about half of Saxe's force had been embarked when a strong British fleet, commanded by Sir John Norris, appeared off the port. An ebb-tide and a dead calm prevented Norris from attacking, but a 'Protestant wind' was no less effective, and that night large numbers of the transports were wrecked or dispersed by a fierce gale, under cover of which the French squadron retired to Brest.

The disaster gave the French Government a convenient excuse for abandoning the project, and although the Prince still remained hopeful of gaining its assistance, his supporters were less sanguine. By the autumn of 1744 even Charles had given up hope, and determining to rely on his fellow-countrymen alone, he informed the Jacobite agent, John Murray of Broughton, that he intended to visit Scotland the following summer.

The Prince's decision was received by the Scottish Jacobites with consternation, most of them considering it 'a mad project', and their alarm was increased when, early in 1745, he gave the date of his arrival as June. Faith in French promises had been badly shaken, and without the visible support of French troops, arms, and money, the Jacobite leaders had no intention of becoming involved in a second 'Fifteen. Early in 1745 a report was accordingly drawn up to dissuade the Prince from sailing, but owing to the dilatoriness of Lord Traquair to whom it had been entrusted, Charles never received it. Meanwhile, knowing nothing of its contents, he completed his preparations, and in June his supporters became 'vastly alarm'd' to hear of his impending arrival.

When, towards the end of July, it became known that the Prince had reached Scotland in a small ship, accompanied by nine* companions, few arms, and little money, the news was received with dismay rather than enthusiasm.

* In addition to the seven usually mentioned, the Prince's companions included Anthony Walsh, owner of the *Du Teillay*, and Buchanan, a messenger.

2

Prologue to the Forty-five

THE PRINCE had had an adventurous voyage. On 5th July he had sailed from Belle Île in the privateer *Du Teillay*, escorted by the French warship *Elizabeth* of 60 guns. One hundred miles west of the Lizard the two ships had been sighted by H.M.S. *Lion*, which engaged the *Elizabeth*, and after a fierce fight, which left both vessels little more than wrecks, the *Du Teillay* sailed on alone.

On 23rd July the Prince set foot for the first time on Scottish soil on the island of Eriskay. It was soon made clear to him that his chances of gaining support were far from hopeful, for MacDonald of Boisdale, a half-brother of the chief of Clanranald, was utterly opposed to his clan taking part in a rising, and added that the Prince could expect no help from the MacDonalds and MacLeods of Skye.

Although shaken by Boisdale's outspokenness, Charles refused to accept defeat, and two days later the *Du Teillay* anchored in Loch nan Uamh, on the coast of Arisaig. Among his earliest visitors was Boisdale's nephew, young Clanranald, who at first was equally against the venture, but eventually promised his clan's support. Similar promises were made by MacDonald of Scotus, representing Glengarry, MacDonald of Keppoch, and MacDonald of Glencoe, but Sir Alexander MacDonald of Sleat and MacLeod of MacLeod refused to call out their men, and had it not been for the powerful support of the Clan Cameron, led by Lochiel, the younger, the Rising would have made little headway.

On 19th August the Prince assembled his army at Glenfinnan, where amidst 'loud huzzas and schiming of bonnetts up into the air', King James' red and white silk standard was unfurled and his commission read appointing Charles as Regent. Among the spectators at this ceremony were the officers and men of two raw companies of the Royal Scots who had been taken prisoner on their way to Fort William.

The Highland army numbered about 1,300 men, and as its Commander-in-Chief the Prince was badly in need of professional advice. With the exception of Keppoch, who had served in the French army, none of the chiefs had received military training, and a senior appointment of any one of them would inevitably have led to friction. Among Charles's oddly-assorted companions in the *Du Teillay* was John William O'Sullivan, a captain in the French service, who was reputed to have some knowledge of staff work, and on the strength of this somewhat doubtful claim the Prince appointed him Quartermaster- and Adjutant-General. It was a singularly unhappy choice, for O'Sullivan's ignorance of his duties was equalled only by his conceit, and few of the Prince's advisers were to exert a more harmful influence over him.

The Prince's time of arrival was well chosen, for the war had stripped the country of troops. In Scotland the Government forces numbered fewer than 4,000 men, excluding the 'invalid' garrisons of Edinburgh, Stirling, and Dumbarton castles, and in quality they were even less impressive.

The infantry consisted of three and a half regiments of the line: Guise's (6th), Murray's (57th), Lascelles's (58th), and five companies of Lee's (55th). There were also nine 'additional' companies, mostly under strength, which had recently been raised for drafting to regiments fighting overseas, and a few, weaker still, belonging to Lord Loudon's new Highland regiment, which was then being recruited. Of these, only Guise's, raised in 1674, could claim to be an 'old' regiment; the others dated only from 1741 and had never been in action. The cavalry, consisting of two dragoon regiments, Gardiner's (13th) and Hamilton's (14th), was similarly untried, for although both had been raised in 1715, neither had since seen service. By a further coincidence both were recruited in Ireland, and not only were their men ill-disciplined but their troop horses were young and untrained to firearms. Weakest of all was the artillery arm, for although there was a sufficient number of guns and mortars in Edinburgh Castle from which to form an adequate field-train, this was offset by the fact that there was not a single royal artillery-man in the whole of Scotland.

Such were the troops under the command of Lieut.-General Sir

John Cope, who seems destined to live for ever as the comic hero of a rousing song. In reality he was far from being the fool and the coward of popular tradition, and had he been given a free hand the Rising might have taken a very different course. As a young officer Cope had served in Spain, and by 1739 he had attained the rank of Major-General, and four years later was present at the battle of Dettingen, receiving the red ribbon of the Bath in recognition of his services. His appointment to the Scottish Command in February 1744 was far from popular in certain military circles in which it was hinted that it had been due to social and political influence rather than to merit. In person he is described as 'a little dressy finical man', but 'easy, well-bred, and affable'.

The political affairs of Scotland were then administered from London by the Secretary of State, Lord Tweeddale, a man of no particular ability. Under his direction at Edinburgh were the law officers of the Crown, known as the 'King's Servants', of whom the senior was the Lord President of the Court of Session, Duncan Forbes of Culloden. Born and bred in the Highlands, Forbes had an unrivalled knowledge of the clans and their complicated family and political ties, and early in July he reported to Cope it was rumoured that the Prince was to land in the Highlands during the summer with the intention of raising an insurrection.

Although Forbes gave the report little credit, Sir John at once forwarded it to Tweeddale, but the King was visiting Hanover, and the Lords Justices, who acted as a regency, did little beyond warning Cope to keep 'a strict Eye' on the Highlands, and avoid alarming the country by taking over-active measures for its safety. On 30th July, a little over three weeks later, the Government received a report that the Prince had actually landed, but so well kept was the secret of his arrival that it was not until 8th August that the first authentic account of it reached Cope from the Highlands.

The plan which he now decided to carry out had been drawn up by him in consultation with Forbes and the rest of the 'King's Servants'. All were agreed that the most effectual means of scotching any projected rising was to crush it 'in the Bud' with as large a force as could be mustered. It would thus not only be possible to disperse any small body of Highlanders already under arms, but the presence of the King's troops would deter others from joining it. There was also reason to believe that, while on the march, Cope's army would be reinforced by men belonging to the 'well-affected' clans. Had he then realised that no such support would be forthcoming, Cope afterwards asserted, he would never have undertaken his march.

Cope's strategy has often been compared unfavourably with that of Argyll during the 'Fifteen, and it has been argued that he should have followed the Duke's example and have concentrated his small force at Stirling behind the defensive barrier of the Forth. To do so is to be wise after the event, for the Prince's arrival without foreign aid contained no suggestion of a formidable insurrection. In any case, to saddle Cope with the entire responsibility for the plan is manifestly unjust, for not only had it Forbes' approval but the unanimous support of the Lords Justices. It was, in fact, owing to their Lordships' insistence that Cope was subsequently to be forced into proceeding with it against his better judgment.

Having chosen Fort Augustus, the fort nearest the disaffected districts, as his objective, Cope ordered all his available troops to assemble at Stirling. For their subsistence large quantities of bread had to be provided, and 'the Ovens at Leith, Stirling, and Perth, were kept at Work Day and Night, Sunday not excepted'. Other supply arrangements included 'a suttler well provided, and a butcher with a drove of black cattle', without which precaution wrote an officer, 'we had starved upon the march'.

Although without royal artillerymen, Cope decided that a 'Show only of some Artillery' might be sufficient to impress the Highlanders, and ordered Mr. Eaglesfield Griffith, Master-Gunner of Edinburgh Castle for the past 30 years, to provide 'a light field train of four $1\frac{1}{2}$-pounders and four coehorn mortars'.* The provision of personnel was less simple, and the best Mr. Griffith could produce were an old man who had served as a gunner in the long defunct 'Scots Train', and three invalids belonging to the garrison of Edinburgh Castle. A more efficient assistant 'in the Business of the Train' was Lieut.-Colonel Whitefoord of Cochran's Marine regiment, who was serving as a volunteer.

While these preparations were proceeding, various conflicting reports continued to reach Cope from the North, including accounts of the landing of French troops. Although some were clearly

---

* Of $4\frac{2}{3}$ inches calibre. Introduced by Coehorn, a celebrated Dutch military engineer.

'inspired', the possibility of a French invasion could not be ignored, and Cope can hardly be blamed for beginning to have second thoughts about leaving Edinburgh and the Lowlands virtually defenceless, especially as he had made it clear from the first that the carrying out of his plan was subject to any later information he might receive.

To Tweeddale and his colleagues, however, any delay by Sir John in putting his plan into operation was completely unacceptable, and he received peremptory orders to march forthwith, 'notwithstanding the Report of the landing of the Troops and even notwithstanding any actual Debarkation of Troops'. In thus insisting that he should carry out his plan regardless of circumstances, the Lords Justices firmly placed the responsibility for its failure on their own shoulders.

The Lords Justices' instructions and a conversation he had had with the Duke of Argyll* can have done little to raise Cope's spirits. In an earlier letter Tweeddale had 'hinted' that should the Duke desire it, he was to be given a supply of arms, but that the offer was to be kept secret to prevent applications being made from less desirable quarters. Far from gratefully accepting it, the chief of the Clan Campbell firmly declined the offer on the ground that it was contrary to the Disarming Act for any of the 'well-affected' clans to appear under arms. It does not seem to have occurred to his Grace that by thus adhering to the letter of the law he was defeating the whole purpose of the Act, for had the Campbells then taken up arms the Rising might well have been still-born. Instead, the Duke departed to London, leaving Cope to comment bitterly to Tweeddale: 'This, my Lord, will shew you, what Assistance I am to expect from the well affected Clans in their present Situation.'

On 20th August Cope set out on his march from Stirling with Murray's regiment, five companies of Lee's, and two 'additional' companies of Lord John Murray's Highlanders, the Black Watch. Next day he was met at Crieff by eight companies of Lascelles's with further supplies of bread. He had 1,000 stands of arms for arming the 'well-affected' Highlanders he expected to join him. Among them were the tenants of the Duke of Atholl and Lord Glenorchy, from both of whom he had received assurances of help. To get round the provisions of the Disarming Act Cope had suggested that their men should enlist for a maximum period of three months, but

* Brother of the Government commander of the '15.

he now found to his dismay that neither nobleman was able to fulfil his undertaking. To save transport he accordingly returned 700 stands of arms to Stirling, and so disgusted was he that had it not been for his 'positive Orders' he would not have marched a step further.

Cope's difficulties increased as the march continued. His baggage horses wandered off during the night, and hours were wasted each morning in trying to round them up; quantities of bread had to be left behind, or were ruined by the wet weather; his Black Watch companies 'mouldered away' by desertion, and reported his movements to the enemy. It was of small consolation that he was joined at Taybridge (Aberfeldy) by a weak company of Lord Loudon's Highlanders.

On 25th August the royal army reached Dalnacardoch, where Cope received his first eye-witness account of the Prince's progress from Captain Sweetenham of Guise's regiment, which was in garrison in the northern forts. Sweetenham who had been taken prisoner, had been dismissed on parole after being present at the standard-raising ceremony at Glenfinnan. He had heard that the Highland army was now about 3,000 strong—about twice its actual strength—and added he had been told that it was intended to oppose Cope's crossing of the Corryarrack Pass over which the road led to Fort Augustus. Next day at Dalwhinnie a letter from Lord President Forbes arrived from Culloden, confirming Sweetenham's report, and at the same time warning Sir John, 'in the most decent Manner his Lordship could think of', of the danger of attempting to force the pass.

Early next morning Cope held a council of war at which it was decided that the march to Fort Augustus was no longer practicable. The alternatives of staying in the neighbourhood of Dalwhinnie, or of retreating to Stirling were then discussed, but the first was clearly out of the question as barely three days' bread supply remained, apart from which there was nothing to prevent the enemy from by-passing the royal army. To retreat to Stirling was not only open to the same objections, but would give encouragement to the wavering clans, and it was unanimously decided to make for Inverness. In addition to ensuring the safety of Fort Augustus and discouraging the rebellious clans from marching southwards, this would afford the 'well affected' an opportunity to join the royal army.

Continuing along the Corryarrack road to conceal his change of plan as long as possible, Cope turned about some three miles short of Garva Bridge, and after rejoining the Inverness road, spent the night at Ruthven. Next day (28th August), having reinforced his army with the company of Guise's stationed in the barrack, and leaving only a sergeant, a corporal, and 12 men to garrison it, Cope pressed on through the dangerous defile of Slochd, and arrived at Inverness on the night of the 29th.

The news of Cope's movements was received by the Highland army leaders with a mixture of elation and disappointment, for having seized the pass on the night of the 26th they had looked forward to giving the royal army an extremely hot reception. Among the small supply of arms landed from the *Du Teillay* was a number of 'swivel guns', and plans had been made to mount them in 'sleeping batteries' so as to enfilade the 17 traverses by which the road wound up the mountain side. It had also been intended to post strong detachments at the top and bottom of the pass, and among the captured Jacobite documents in the 'Cumberland Papers' is a memorandum in O'Sullivan's handwriting endorsed 'rebels order of Battle Aug 28 1745'. At this early stage in the campaign it shows the MacDonalds were willing to leave it to chance to decide which clan regiment occupied the post of honour on the right of the line.

It was at first suggested that the royal army should be pursued and brought to action, but on second thoughts it seemed foolish not to take advantage of the open door to the Lowlands, and marching by way of Dalnacardoch, Blair Atholl, and Dunkeld, the Highland army entered Perth on 4th September. Meanwhile Cope had found a further disappointment awaiting him at Inverness, for in spite of the help of Lord President Forbes, the only clan willing to offer him immediate support were the Munros. Of the rest, some of their chiefs pled the delay involved in raising their men; others, the danger of exposing their countries to their Jacobite neighbours. For a couple of days after his arrival Cope was uncertain of the Prince's intentions, but a dispatch received on 31st August from the sergeant in charge at Ruthven Barrack, reporting that he had been attacked, dispelled all doubt. It was to be a race for the Lowlands, and having hastily ordered shipping to be sent from Leith to Aberdeen to carry his army southwards, Cope marched from Inverness on 4th September. Before leaving, he replaced one of his Black Watch companies with a company of Guise's from Fort George, with the addition of two half-formed companies of Lord Loudon's Highlanders, two more 1½-pounders and two royal (5½-inch) mortars. He was joined by another company of Loudon's at Aberdeen.

The two dragoon regiments, which Cope had left in the Lowlands owing to the difficulty of obtaining forage, were now the only regular troops opposing the Highland army, Gardiner's being stationed at Stirling and Hamilton's at Edinburgh. In command of the former was Colonel James Gardiner, who as a dashing young cavalryman had been equally famed for his skill in breaking horses and female hearts. He had fought with great bravery at Preston in the 'Fifteen, where it was said that 'his language seemed to rend the Heavens' and shocked even some of his brother-officers. Some years later, as the result of a religious awakening, he had become a changed man, and although his courage remained unaltered, he had acquired a narrow and fatalistic outlook. This state of mind had lately become intensified by a severe illness, and both mentally and physically Gardiner was quite unfit for active service.

In Cope's absence the two regiments were under the operational command of Lieut.-General Joshua Guest, the senior officer in the Lowlands, who was stationed at Edinburgh. Aged 85, Guest was, in fact, a very senior officer indeed, and although said to be 'very alert', he had an old man's dislike of having to make a decision, a thing he was now called upon to do.

Cope's urgent request for shipping had reached him on 4th September—the same day as the Highland army entered Perth—and being thus aware of Cope's plans and the speed of the Prince's advance, Guest was faced with two obvious alternatives. He could order Hamilton's regiment to reinforce Gardiner's at Stirling or withdraw Gardiner's to Edinburgh. The first had the approval of Gardiner and of Major-General Blakeney, who commanded the garrison of Stirling Castle, but Guest may have considered that before doing so it might be safer to await the arrival of a Dutch infantry regiment, which was expected hourly at Leith. Knowing, too, that Edinburgh was far from being whole-heartedly Whig, he may also have felt it necessary to keep Hamilton's close at hand to preserve order. What he failed to realise was the danger of dividing his troops, and the folly of leaving Gardiner's 'in the air'. In the event, as Guest should have foreseen, Gardiner's was incapable of holding up the Highland army single-handed, and having been recently at grass was in no fit state for heavy duty.

The Highland army remained at Perth for a week gathering reinforcements. It was joined there by James Drummond, titular 3rd Duke of Perth, and Lord George Murray, whom the Prince appointed his Lieutenant-Generals. They presented a remarkable contrast. Perth, a man of 32 and a Roman Catholic, had been brought up in France, where he had acquired a smattering of military engineering. Since his return to Scotland in his late teens he had lived with his mother at Drummond Castle, near Crieff. Agriculture and horse-racing were among his interests and shortly before the outbreak of the Rising he had narrowly escaped arrest on account of his Jacobite activities. Although physically far from strong, Perth was not only brave, but became universally popular in the Highland army on account of his modesty and kind-heartedness. He was also slow to take offence, a quality which later proved most valuable in working with Murray.

Born in 1694, Lord George had held a regular commission at the time of the 'Fifteen, but with his two elder brothers he had joined the Jacobite army. Four years later with his brother, Tullibardine, he had been present at Glenshiel, and after six years of exile had been pardoned. After returning home he had settled down to the peaceful life of a happily-married country-gentleman, and his decision to share the Prince's fortunes was dictated solely by a sense of duty. He was to receive little thanks in return, for having latterly lived on friendly terms with his Whig brother, James, Duke of Atholl, and Government supporters like Lord President Forbes, the Prince from the very first suspected his loyalty. Encouraged by Charles's secretary, Murray of Broughton, this baseless suspicion, combined with Lord George's blunt and sometimes overbearing manner, bedevilled their relationship. Yet to no man did the Prince owe more, for although junior in seniority to Perth, Lord George's outstanding ability and strength of character were to make him the mainspring of the Highland army.

Continuing its southward advance, the Highland army left Perth on 11th September, and two days later crossed the Forth at the Fords of Frew, eight miles above Stirling. Not a dragoon was to be seen, for although Gardiner had spoken of giving the Highlanders 'a

1   Prince Charles Edward (From a contemporary engraving)

2 Field-Marshal George Wade (From a drawing by Alexander van Haeken after the portrait by Vanderbank)

3 The Duke of Atholl (From a contemporary drawing)

4   The Earl of Loudon
(From the portrait by Allan
Ramsay)

5   Duncan Forbes of Culloden (From a
portrait attributed to Jeremiah Davison)

6 'The Scottish Camp': an imaginative view of the Highland army's camp at Edinburgh (From a contemporary engraving)

7 Viscount Strathallan
(From a contemporary
portrait)

8 Lord Nairne (From
the portrait by Jeremiah
Davison)

9 'The Invasion or Perkins Triumph': a warning to Protestants against Popery (From a satirical print of September 1745)

10 'A Race from Preston Pans to Berwick': Sir John Cope brings the news of his own defeat (From a contemporary satirical print)

11 Lord Ogilvy (From the portrait by Allan Ramsay)

12 Lord Elcho (From the portrait by John Alexander)

13 Alexander Robertson of Struan (From a contemporary portrait)

14 Lord Lovat (From the portrait by William Hogarth)

warm reception', he made no attempt to delay their progress, but retired with his regiment to Falkirk. He seems to have had a presentiment of his approaching end, for when his wife, who was staying at Stirling, showed unusual emotion in parting from him, he said only: 'We have an Eternity to spend together.'

The day after crossing the Forth the Highland army marched on to Falkirk, while Gardiner and his men retreated to Linlithgow. At Falkirk the Prince stayed at Callendar House with the ill-fated Earl of Kilmarnock, who earlier that day had dined with Gardiner's officers. Hearing from them that they intended to defend Linlithgow Bridge, the Earl passed on this information to the Jacobite leaders, and at 1 o'clock the following morning Lord George Murray set out with 1,000 men in hopes of taking the dragoons by surprise. On arriving at Linlithgow, however, he found that they had retreated a few hours earlier towards Edinburgh, and the same day (15th September) the Prince pushed on to Kirkliston, while Gardiner fell back on Corstorphine, three miles west of the city. There he was joined by Hamilton's in company with a few hundred men of the newly-formed Edinburgh regiment and the Town Guard, and, having posted a rear-guard, both dragoon regiments retired for the night to a field near the Colt Bridge.

That evening Brigadier Thomas Fowke arrived at Edinburgh from England. He had been sent to take command of the dragoons and the long-awaited Dutch infantry regiment, and early the next morning he reviewed the two dragoon regiments at their camp. They were drawn up with Gardiner at their head, 'muffled in a wide blue surcoat, with a handkerchief drawn round his hat, and tied under his chin'. His officers and men presented an equally unsoldier-like appearance. 'I found', reported the Brigadier, '. . . many of the Men's and some of the Officers Legs so swell'd, that they could not wear Boots; and those who really were to be depended upon, in a manner overcome for want of Sleep.' Nor were the horses in better condition, for having been recently at grass they were 'soft', and many of their backs were 'not fit to receive the Riders'. Gardiner's state of mind was equally depressing. According to Captain Singleton, Fowke's Brigade-Major, he:

'represented to the Brigadier very strongly, and repeated many times . . . the bad Condition his Regiment was in; in particular being harass'd and fatigued for eleven Days and eleven Nights, little or no

Provision for the Men, or Forage for the Horses . . . and that if they stay'd another Night on that Ground, it was to be feared his Majesty would lose two Regiments of Dragoons; But added, the Brigadier might do as he pleased; for his Part he had not long to live.'

On being informed of this unfortunate state of affairs Guest recommended that both regiments should retire so as to be in readiness to join Cope's army which was expected to arrive at any moment, and it was decided to withdraw them to Leith links. Soon afterwards the rear-guard at Corstorphine reported that the Highland army was beginning to advance, and according to popular tradition it was this party which was responsible for starting what became known as the 'Coltbrig Canter'. For on being fired on by a few Highland gentlemen armed with pistols it is said to have fallen back in panic on the main body, whereupon both regiments galloped off along the 'Lang Dykes', the line of the present-day Princes Street. On the other hand, Fowke's evidence given at his subsequent examination, and confirmed by that of other officers, contains not the least suggestion of alarm, and stresses the fact that the dragoons' withdrawal was 'regularly performed'. It is possible that both accounts contain a modicum of truth, and although Fowke and the leading squadrons moved off slowly, those in rear may have had to break into a canter from time to time in order to keep up with them.

Edinburgh was now in a state of panic-stricken uproar, some of the citizens demanding that the town should be defended, others that it should be surrendered to prevent useless loss of life. In the centre of this hurly-burly was the unfortunate Lord Provost, Archibald Stewart, on whom the Crown lawyers and Guest—all safely out of harm's way—sought to shift responsibility by making separate offers of the assistance of the dragoons. These Stewart adroitly countered by replying, in effect, that if they considered such help desirable, they would no doubt issue the appropriate orders; for his part he 'would neither bid nor forbid them . . .'. To add to the confusion, a summons arrived from the Prince, calling on the town to capitulate, closely followed by the news that Cope's transports had been sighted in the Firth. This news came too late, for it had been decided to open negotiations with the Prince, and a deputation from the Town Council was on its way to his camp at Slateford.

Meanwhile, having been unable to obtain forage at Leith, the dragoons had withdrawn to Musselburgh, where they were equally unsuccessful, and on Gardiner's suggestion they pushed on to Prestonpans, which adjoined his little estate of Bankton. The Colonel preceded them to make supply arrangements, and being 'very ill and extreamly weak', was given permission by Fowke to spend the night in his own house. On arriving there about 8 o'clock he retired to bed, but was not left long undisturbed, for two hours later he was roused by his Adjutant, Cornet Ker, who reported that the dragoons had taken the alarm, and were about to ride off. Two explanations are given for the cause of their panic. According to tradition, a dragoon, in search of forage, fell into a disused coal-pit, whence his cries for help led his comrades to believe that the High-landers were upon them. A more probable explanation is that the alarm was raised by the country-people, who objected to their supplies of hay being requisitioned.

Many of the dragoon officers were on the point of sitting down to supper in a tavern at Prestonpans when the alarm broke out, and despite the assurance of young Alexander Carlyle, the minister's son, who had just arrived from Edinburgh, that no Highlanders were on the march, they refused to believe him. 'It was vain to tell them that the rebels had neither wings nor horses, nor were invisible. Away they went as fast as they could to their corps.' The camp was a scene of confusion. Most of the men had bridled up, and some had mounted, whereupon Fowke 'ordered them all to mount and march off in good Order'. So far were his instructions from being obeyed that next morning the road taken by the dragoons was littered with pistols, swords, and other equipment, and during the night they became separated into two bodies, the one proceeding to North Berwick, and the other to Dunbar, where Cope's army was about to disembark.

Sir John was just too late, for while his little fleet had been slowly reaching across the Firth in the darkness, a second Town Council deputation was returning to Edinburgh from the Highland army's camp, where the Prince had curtly refused to consider a plea for further time to discuss terms of surrender. After dropping the deputation at a tavern its hackney-coach set out for its stables in the Canongate, and on arriving at the Netherbow Port the gate was opened to let it pass. No sooner had this been done than a detach-ment of Highlanders led by Lochiel and O'Sullivan, which had been lying in wait outside, rushed in and disarmed the volunteer guard without the least resistance. By the early hours of the morning the whole city was in Jacobite hands, and so quietly was its seizure effected that when later in the day a citizen saw a Highlander sitting on one of the captured guns, he remarked innocently '"that surely these were not the same troops which mounted guard yesterday." "Och, no", replied the Highlander, "she pe relieved."'

A Highland Gentleman
From an engraving after a
contemporary drawing

3

Prestonpans

A MESSENGER carrying the news of Edinburgh's capture was sent off by boat to Cope from Dunbar, and on landing there a few hours later Sir John was soon in possession of the most up-to-date reports. He had no lack of informants, for the little port was crowded with visitors who had come to watch his army disembark. Among them were such prominent Government supporters as the Lord Advocate, the Lord Justice-Clerk, the Solicitor-General, and several judges, and they included also many of the volunteers who had tried unsuccessfully to defend the city.

Marching without a day's halt, Cope had reached Aberdeen on 11th September, where he received the welcome news that an officer of the Royal Artillery and 17 gunners and matrosses* had arrived at Edinburgh from Woolwich. He had accordingly sent orders that they were to join him at his landing-place, but he now found to his disappointment that none had turned up. Guest's failure to supply them appears inexcusable, for the Castle was in no danger of attack, and knowing Cope's dire need of the men there was nothing to have prevented him from sending them off immediately the fall of the city was seen to be inevitable. Meanwhile, having again written to Guest in the hope that the party might somehow manage to join him, Cope borrowed six seaman-gunners from H.M. ships *Fox* and *Hazard*, which had convoyed his transports from Aberdeen. They were to prove more of a liability than an asset, for according to Lieut.-Colonel Whitefoord they 'were generally drunk upon the March; and upon the Day of Action, ran

---

* 'Soldiers belonging to the Artillery, next under the Gunners, whom they are to assist in traversing, sponging, loading and firing the Guns, &c.' *The News-Readers Pocket-Book*, 1759.

away before the Action begun; and he could never have any Dependance upon them during the two Days they were with him'.

Although greatly disappointed that he had arrived too late to save Edinburgh, Cope was determined to bring the enemy to action at the earliest possible moment. By the evening of Tuesday, 17th September, the infantry and most of the artillery had been got ashore, and the disembarkation was completed the following afternoon, but because the dragoons were 'so fatigued they could not march', the army remained at Dunbar overnight. As a cavalryman, the condition in which the two regiments had joined him cannot have escaped Cope's eye, but possibly in deference to the memory of Gardiner, he made little reference to it at his 'Examination'. Gardiner himself, as Fowke's Brigade-Major testified, had no such inhibitions, and while at Dunbar he expressed his views to at least two of his acquaintances with the greatest of freedom.

One of them was General Lord Mark Kerr, who, finding that he had arrived too late to take up his command as Governor of Edinburgh Castle, was on his way back to Berwick. Having been one of Cope's unsuccessful rivals for the post of Commander-in-Chief, although 'very solicitous to have it', he was probably a not unsympathetic listener. He wrote:

'Upon my getting there [Dunbar], I met with Coll: Gardner who complain'd much of the retreat, I may say run a way, of the two Reg^ts. of Dragoons from the neighbourhood of Edinburgh, which he said had ruin'd his Reg^t., were his Words. And in conversation with my old Acquaintance he said that there has been the oddest proceedings and Blunders that ever were heard of, these were his Words. I ask'd him what he believed would be their Operations now; he said he believed Sir Jno Cope would fight to retrieve what had been past, upon which I shak'd my Head, but really don't remember what I said, but Coll Gardner added he believed they should beat them. I had no sooner shifted than I found Sir Jno Cope standing by me, he complain'd that the Rebels would get both Arms and Ammunition by being in Possession of Edinburgh. He communicated nothing more to me, and I having no Power to Command bid God bless them and set out.'

Cope, as he well knew, had other enemies besides the Jacobites.

Later the same day young Carlyle visited the Colonel, who was staying with the minister of Dunbar. Before dinner they walked in the manse garden, and Carlyle describes him as looking

'pale and dejected, which I attributed to his bad health, and the fatigue he had lately undergone. I began to ask him if he was not now satisfied with the junction of the foot and the dragoons, and confident that they would give account of the rebels. He answered dejectedly that he hoped it might be so, but—and then made a long pause. I said, that to be sure they had made a very hasty retreat; 'a foul flight', said he, 'Sandie, and they have not recovered from their panic; and I'll tell you in confidence that I have not above ten men in my regiment whom I am certain will follow me. But we must give them battle now, and God's will be done!' '

During dinner with the minister's family and his relative, Cornet Ker, Gardiner 'assumed an air of gaiety', and joked with Carlyle about his adventures as a volunteer, and his rawness as a soldier in not having taken up the first good quarters he could find the previous night. As for the coming battle, the Colonel spoke of it as a certain victory, 'if God were on our side'.

Another young man, John Home, destined to become better known as the author of *Douglas* ('Whaur's yer Wullie Shakespeare noo?'), and a history of the Rising, was also a volunteer with the royal army. He had arrived that day from Edinburgh, and was able to give Cope a singularly detailed account of the Highland army and its numbers. After making a round of the various enemy-held posts in the city, Home had gone out to the King's Park where the main body of the Highland army was encamped, and on arriving there had found the men 'sitting in ranks upon the ground, extremely intent upon their food'. So intent were they that he had been able to count them 'man by man', and after including those in the city, he reckoned the Highlanders' numbers to amount to fewer than 2,000 men. In appearance he noted that 'most of them seemed to be strong, active, and hardy men' of average build, whose Highland dress set off their figures to advantage, and that 'their stern countenances, and bushy uncombed hair, gave them a fierce, barbarous, and imposing aspect'. Although three-quarters of them were armed with swords and fire-locks, the latter were 'of all sorts and sizes, muskets, fusees, and fowling-pieces'; of the rest, some had only a sword or a firelock, and he had noticed about a hundred men who were armed with scythe-blades attached to pitchfork shafts. As for artillery he had seen only 'one small iron gun . . . without a carriage, lying upon a cart, drawn by a little Highland horse'.

On the morning of the 19th the royal army began its advance on Edinburgh. Led by Lord John Murray's and Lord Loudon's Highlanders in their dark tartans, the long red column with its train of artillery and baggage waggons 'extended for several miles along the road'. Accompanying it were large numbers of country-people attracted by the unusual spectacle, and had Hogarth been present he would have found ample material for a companion-piece to his 'March to Finchley'. Although many followed the army solely out of curiosity, there were others who were prompted by less innocent motives, for according to Carlyle 'many people in East Lothian at that time were Jacobites, and they were most forward to mix with the soldiers'. In contrast Cope did his best to improve his troops' morale, and 'all along on the March, by riding through the Ranks, and encouraging the Men, he . . . raised their Spirits to such a Degree, that all express'd the strongest Desire for Action; even the Dragoons breath'd nothing but Revenge, and threaten'd the Rebels with nothing but Destruction'.

Cope had intended to push on as far as possible, but having covered the 11 miles to Haddington by the early afternoon, and finding that there was an insufficient supply of water for some considerable distance further on, he decided to remain there until next day. A camp was formed to the west of the town, and the officers crowded hopefully into the inns in search of dinner, but before they had time to sit down to a meal the drums beat to arms, and they had to hurry back to their regiments. It was soon discovered to be a false alarm, which, it was alleged, had 'followed' the coach carrying the Hon. Francis Charteris and his newly-wedded wife to their home nearby, and this rumour may well have been true. For not only was his bride a daughter of the dowager Duchess of Gordon, who had Jacobite sympathies, but his elder brother, Lord Elcho, was with the Prince, and he himself had subscribed towards the Cause. In any event the incident can have done little to increase Cope's confidence in his men, but to gloss over it he thanked them for their alertness, on which they returned him 'an huzza'.

Among the 80 or so volunteers who had joined the royal army were a number of students from the College of Edinburgh, who, like Carlyle and Home, had belonged to the volunteer company commanded by ex-Lord Provost George Drummond. On Cope's suggestion 16 of them were detailed to reconnoitre the roads to the west of Haddington during the night, and having been divided into two shifts they were sent off in pairs, mounted on post-horses. All returned to report that everything was quiet, excepting one pair, who were taken prisoner by a Jacobite patrol while they were enjoying an early morning meal of oysters and white wine at an inn near Musselburgh. After having been threatened with hanging as spies, or, alternatively, with being placed in the forefront of the battle, they were released the following afternoon through the good offices of a Jacobite fellow-student.

One volunteer whose services Cope must subsequently have regretted accepting was a certain Richard Jack, who claimed to be 'a Professor of Mathematicks' and to have made 'some Improvements in Gunnery'. Of the 40-odd witnesses who testified at Sir John's 'Examination', Jack's was the only hostile evidence, and so ridiculous are some of his allegations that it is difficult to avoid the suspicion that he was briefed to throw as much mud as possible in the hope that some of it might stick. On the other hand his so-called evidence is of value in elucidating certain points which might otherwise have remained obscure.

As the royal army now included the two dragoon regiments, a new 'Order of Battle' was drawn up and issued to the commanding officers by Lord Loudon, the Adjutant-General. Like others of that date it displayed the same regard for symmetry that is to be found in the final line-up of a Christmas pantomime.

GENERAL Sir John Cope
BRIGADIER Fowke

Colonel Gardener				Colonel Lascells
2 Sq. Drags.	2ps. Can.	2ps. Can.	2ps. Can.	2 Sq. Drags.
	Murray's	Lascells's, Lee's	and Cohorns	

Corps de Reserve

1 Squad. Drag.	Highlanders, Volunteers	1 Squad. Drag.

In the forthcoming battle this 'Order' was, for various reasons, to undergo considerable alteration.

At 9 o'clock the following morning (20th September), the royal army set out from Haddington on the next stage of its advance. Marching for the first few miles by the Edinburgh post-road, it turned off northwards half-way between Haddington and Tranent and joined the road running west from Longniddry to Preston. In contrast to the post-road, which on approaching Tranent climbed upwards along the shoulder of a ridge, this road passed through open, level, country, and involved the making of a considerable detour. In choosing this lower and more roundabout route Cope, perhaps unwittingly, showed not a little foresight. He was, as yet, uncertain of the enemy's movements, and although the post-road possessed certain obvious advantages, the country through which it ran in the neighbourhood of Tranent was intersected by enclosures, hollow roads, and coal pits, 'where our Horse could not act, and which we could not get pass'd before the Rebels might come up to us . . .'. As coming events were to show, his choice was the correct one.

Having covered about eight miles the royal army halted near the village of St. Germains, and Lord Loudon, Lieut.-Colonel White-foord, and Major Caulfeild, the Quartermaster-General, rode forward to select a camp site near Pinkie. They were accompanied by Lord Home, a Captain in the 3rd Dragoon Guards, who was serving as a volunteer, and Lord Drummore, who, although a middle-aged judge, was an enthusiastic camp-follower. If, like many of Cope's officers, they believed that the Highland army would not dare to face the royal troops, they were soon to be disillusioned, for on approaching Musselburgh the Highlanders came into view 'in full march towards them'.

Following upon the capture of Edinburgh, the Prince had spent three busy days. A few hours after its surrender he had ridden into the city from his camp at Slateford and, attended by the Duke of Perth and Lord Elcho, had made his triumphal entry into the ancient Palace of Holyroodhouse, surrounded by cheering crowds of spectators. The Prince, 'smiling all the Time', was much pleased by his reception, and long after the greater part of the world had forgotten him and his Cause, he must often have harked back in memory to the events of that exciting day. An eye-witness wrote:

'He was a tall slender young Man, about five Feet ten Inches high, of a ruddy Complexion, high nosed, large rolling brown Eyes, long visaged, red-haired, but at that Time wore a pale Periwig. He was in Highland Habit, had a blue Sash, wrought with Gold, that came over his Shoulder; red Velvet Breeches, a green Velvet Bonnet, with a white Cockade, and a Gold Lace about it. He had a Silver-hilted broad Sword, and was shewn great Respect by his Forces.'

Later that morning, at the city Cross, the Heralds—under duress —proclaimed his Majesty King James the Eighth, but some who heard them must have been struck by a sense of unreality as they listened to the words, 'King of Scotland, England, France, and Ireland . . .', for high overhead the Union Flag still floated defiantly above the Castle ramparts. Deeds, not words, could alone make good *that* claim.

The news that Cope was disembarking his army at Dunbar was greeted by the Prince with, 'Is he, by God?', a remark of Wellingtonian brevity, and hurried steps were taken to remedy some of the Highland army's more obvious deficiencies. Arms and ammunition were its most urgent requirements, and a proclamation demanding their surrender succeeded in bringing in about 1,200 muskets, either 'good or indifferent', and some powder and ball. Apart from smallarms there was little military equipment of value, for the cannon brought up from Leith to defend the city were useless for field work, being mounted on heavy, small-wheeled carriages; in any case there were as yet no artillerymen in the Jacobite army.

On the 19th the Highland main body, which had been bivouacking in the King's Park, moved off to a new camp near Duddingston. The Prince and his principal officers took up quarters in the village, and at a council of war that evening it was decided that instead of awaiting the royal army's approach the Highland army should march boldly forward to meet it.

Almost as important a decision to be made was which regiment should have the honour of being posted on the right of the front line in the forthcoming action, a matter that was to prove a bone of contention to the very end of the campaign. For although, as already mentioned, a scheme of drawing lots had apparently been agreed upon a month before, the MacDonalds again brought up the controversial subject, and the Prince becoming 'difficulted' sent for Lord George Murray to try to settle the dispute. This he proceeded to do in his usual practical way. He said:

'In an army such as theirs he did not see how any Regiment or name [the Macdonalds were those who made the greatest demure] could claim a right before another. If they were to be ruled by precedents he could show that the Athollmen had always the right in Montrose's Army. But he thought the agreement they had come to and observed since the first setting up of the Standard was a very right one and should be the rule. They took the van alternatively; so whosoever turn it was to have the front were to have the right that day if a battle should happen.'

Although differing from the previous scheme of drawing lots, Lord George's similarly set aside the claim of any one clan to occupy the coveted position. Yet such was his eloquence that it was at once suggested that the Athollmen should be given the honour in the coming battle, but Murray declined it on the ground that as they were poorly armed it would be better that they should be posted in the reserve. His proposal was accordingly agreed to, with only one dissentient. This was Sir John MacDonald, an Irish captain in the Spanish service, and a crony of O'Sullivan's, who declared 'that if he had any command amongst the Macdonalds none should have the right but them'.

At the same meeting the Prince asked the chiefs how they thought their men would behave in action against regular troops, and Keppoch was called upon by them to give his opinion. He replied that as hardly any of the men had been in action before it was difficult to say, but that loving the Prince's cause and their chiefs as they did, he had no doubt that they would follow their officers. Charles then announced that he himself would lead them, and charge at their head, but not surprisingly the chiefs were dismayed by this rash suggestion. If anything happened to him, they declared, 'defeat or victory was the same to them', and they threatened to return home with their men unless he withdrew his proposal. This fact is worth remembering, for although the Prince's courage has sometimes been questioned, it is clear that it was solely in deference to the chieftains' wishes that in the two earlier battles of the 'Forty-Five he posted himself in rear.

During the night of the 19th mounted patrols were sent out to reconnoitre the roads leading towards Musselburgh, but beyond the capture of Cope's student volunteers they had nothing to report. Orders had been given that all the command-posts in Edinburgh were to be evacuated, and early on the morning of the 20th the detachments which had been holding them rejoined the Highland main body. In addition to the five clan regiments which had joined him soon after his arrival, the Prince's army now included the men of other clans who had been recruited during its southward advance. Among them were the Robertsons, Menzies's, and MacGregors, and others like the MacLachlans, who had arrived later from further afield. There were, too, the tenants of Perthshire landowners, such as Lord Nairne and Oliphant of Gask, few of whom showed any great enthusiasm for the Cause, and even William Murray—in Jacobite eyes the rightful Duke of Atholl—was hard put to it to raise his Whig brother's men. Except for a small body of between 30 and 40 mounted troops commanded by William Drummond, Lord Strathallan, the Prince was without cavalry, and his whole force —like Cope's—numbered approximately 2,550* men.

Reports now began to come in that the royal army was about to march from Haddington, and amid the skirling pipes the High-landers hurried to join their regiments, falling-in as usual in three ranks. When the men were assembled the Prince called the chiefs together and made them a short speech. Everything, he said, had been arranged and agreed upon, and all now depended on their order and conduct. He wished for success as much on their account as on that of his father or his own, so that they might be delivered from their present slavery, and reminded them that they were fighting for a good cause, unlike their enemies, who by the knowledge that they were fighting against their King and country would be already half-defeated. Finally, drawing his sword, he exclaimed dramatically: 'Gentlemen, I have flung away the scabbard; with God's help I will make you a free and happy people!' On his words being repeated to the men, 'all the Bonnets were in the Air, & such a Cry, yt it wou'd be wherewithall to frighten any enemy . . .'. The Prince then raised his hand in signal, and the Highland army marched off.

It was now between 9 and 10 o'clock, and led by Lord George Murray, with Lochiel and his Camerons in the van, the Highlanders in one long column of threes made their way eastwards towards Musselburgh. Ahead of them Lord Strathallan's troopers rode for-ward as an advance-guard, but so rapid was the movement of the main body that it had crossed the old bridge over the Esk at Mussel-burgh, and had reached a point a little to the south of Pinkie House

*Based on W. B. Blaikie's figures in his *Itinerary of Prince Charles Edward Stuart,* pp. 90-91.

before the advance-guard's first report of the enemy's motions was received. This contained the information that parties of dragoons had been observed in the neighbourhood of Preston, and that the rest of the royal army could not be far away. The report added that it seemed probable that Cope would attempt to seize the high ground to the west of Tranent, known as Falside Hill.

Lord George at once determined to forestall any such attempt. Not only did he know the country well, but he was equally aware of the value which the Highlanders attached to an elevated position. Judging by the report there was not a moment to be lost, and without wasting time in discussion, or in waiting for orders from Perth or the Prince, he struck off the road in an easterly direction across the fields. Marching to the south of the village of Walliford, the Highlanders began to breast the slopes of Falside Hill, and so fast a pace was set by the van that the rear of the column had almost to break into a run to keep up with it. Soon glimpses were to be seen of the coastal plain below them to the northward, and within half an hour the leading regiments had gained the top of the hill, when Lord George slackened speed. Moving along the crest-line the head of the column rejoined the post-road about half a mile to the west of Tranent, and now, little more than three-quarters of a mile off and a hundred feet below, could be clearly seen the royal army drawn up in order of battle. It was a long-awaited moment, and the two armies greeted each other with a volley of shouts.

After sighting the Highland army near Musselburgh, Lord Loudon, followed by the rest of the officers, had galloped back to warn Cope of its approach. On their return about noon they found the royal advance-guard at the eastern end of a flat and featureless tract of ground lying to the north of the higher land around Tranent. Running east and west, it was about a mile and a half in length by three-quarters of a mile in width, and entirely open and without cover of any sort. Part of it had been under corn and was now covered with stubble, and Cope was not long in deciding that here was the ideal field of battle. 'There is not', he afterwards wrote, 'in the whole of the Ground between Edinburgh and Dunbar a better Spot for both Horse and Foot to act upon.'

The position was well protected on three sides. To the north was the sea, and the villages of Port Seton, Cockenzie, and Prestonpans, while forming a barrier extending half-way along its western boundary, were the ten-foot park walls surrounding Preston House and grounds. Immediately in rear of Preston House was Colonel Gardiner's estate of Bankton, while to the east of the Colonel's enclosures, and flanking almost the whole of the south side of the position, was a stretch of marshy ground known as 'Tranent Meadows'. Although some of this land had been partially drained and divided into small enclosures surrounded by hedges and dry-stone dykes, much the greater part of it was a deep morass from which the surplus water was carried off by a series of ditches. The largest of these, some 8 feet wide and 4 feet deep, formed the southern boundary of the position for nearly three-quarters of its length. From the so-called 'meadows' the ground sloped gently upwards to the ridge on which stood the village of Tranent, a huddle of mean little houses inhabited by the colliers who worked in the surrounding pits.

There were two tracks through what Home calls 'this uncouth piece of ground' separating the two armies. One was 'the waggon way', a primitive railway with wooden rails, along which coal was trundled in horse-drawn waggons from the pits around Tranent to Cockenzie. Descending through a wooded gully called 'The Heugh', immediately to the west of Tranent churchyard, it traversed the morass, and after crossing the large ditch ran north-wards across the plain towards the sea. The other, a cart road running farther to the east, crossed 'the waggon way' near the centre of the plain, and likewise terminated at Cockenzie. To Cope neither was a danger as a possible line of attack, for both were narrow and easily guarded.

On the east Cope's position was comparatively open, excepting for the enclosures surrounding the ruins of Seton Tower, and the cottages of Seton village.

From Loudon's report it seemed certain that the Highlanders' approach would be from the west, and having advanced towards the centre of the plain, Cope drew up his army facing south-west, with the baggage in rear. In this position he was able to command the only approaches, either to the north of Preston park walls, or through a narrow defile running between the Preston and Bankton estates. He was still without regular gunners, and for this reason the artillery, instead of being distributed throughout the line, was posted all together on the left wing.

It was now nearly 2 p.m., and soon afterwards the Highland army came into view on the brow of Falside Hill, very much further to the southward than Cope had expected. From the army's subsequent movements its objective was evidently the high ground to the south overlooking his position, and satisfied that all danger of an attack from the west was at an end, Cope changed front. The position he now took up in the same order of battle was considerably nearer the enemy, with his line running parallel to the ditch, his right towards Preston park walls, and his left towards Seton village.

Cope had no reason for anxiety; instead, the boot was on the other leg, for having gained the higher ground, the Jacobite leaders now found it to be of little advantage to them. On completion of its march the Highland army had taken up position on a line running westwards along the ridge from the outskirts of Tranent to a point overlooking Bankton House, the van being now the right of the line, and the rear the left. At first sight nothing appeared easier than to charge downhill on the enemy—the Highlanders' traditional method of attack—but on closer inspection the 'Tranent Meadows' turned out to be a singularly unsuitable no-man's land over which to advance. Local opinion strongly supported this view, but to make assurance doubly sure, Lord George Murray sent off Colonel Ker of Graden, an officer who had seen service in the Spanish army, to examine the ground in detail. This he proceeded to do, mounted on 'a little white pony'. Although fired on by some of Cope's men, he coolly disregarded their musket-balls, and at one point dismounted, and having pulled down part of a dry-stone dyke, led his pony over it. On returning he reported to Lord George that any attack on the royal army from this direction was quite impracticable.

Cope has been accused by Sir Walter Scott, among others, of confining his army in 'a pinfold' of ground, but to Lord George Murray and the other Jacobite leaders his position appeared in a very different light. 'Very strong' (Murray); 'Very good' (O'Sullivan); 'Chosen with a great deal of skill' (Johnstone); are some of their comments, and Johnstone, who as aide-de-camp to Lord George must have been especially well informed, gives a vivid summing-up of the Jacobites' dilemma: 'We spent the afternoon in reconnoitring his position; and the more we examined it, the more our uneasiness and chagrin increased, as we saw no possibility of attacking it, without exposing ourselves to be cut to pieces in a disgraceful manner.'

During this period of indecision there is no record of the Highland army's commanders having met to discuss what was to be done; on the contrary, the Prince and Lord George Murray appear to have acted quite independently of each other. Lord George, indeed, seems to have deliberately avoided Charles, for knowing that O'Sullivan had his ear, he had probably no wish to be drawn into discussing some hare-brained scheme inspired by the Adjutant-General. On his part O'Sullivan, as a professional soldier, was equally critical of Lord George, some of whose ideas seemed to him to outrage accepted military practice, and the events of this afternoon were to provide a foretaste of the mistrust and ill-feeling that were to subsist between the two men throughout the campaign.

Although there was little danger of a frontal attack by the royal army, out-guards were posted in advance of the Highland position. One of the largest of these parties was stationed at the Heugh, but apparently considering that it required to be reinforced, O'Sullivan ordered 50 of Lochiel's regiment to occupy the adjacent churchyard, 'for what reason', wrote Lord George Murray, 'I could not understand'.

Shortly afterwards, according to O'Sullivan, Lord George and the Prince were involved in a deplorable scene. As it seemed possible that Cope, instead of fighting, might attempt to slip away towards Edinburgh during the night, the Prince had given orders that the Athollmen, who formed part of the reserve under Lord Nairne, were to take up a position covering the roads leading to Musselburgh. News of this movement had evidently reached Lord George from unofficial sources, for on the Prince coming over to the right he asked him 'in a very high tone, what was become of the Athol Brigade; the Prince told him, upon wch Ld George threw his gun on the Ground in a great passion, & Swore God, he'd never draw his sword for the cause, if the Bregade was not brought back'. In face of this outburst the Prince meekly agreed to cancel the order, but having been 'brought to himself' by Lochiel, Lord George later asked that it might stand.

O'Sullivan's account, which is the sole record of this incident, suggests that as commander of the Athollmen, Lord George had no intention of letting them be ordered about without his knowledge and consent, but knowing that they were badly-armed, Murray may not unreasonably have considered them unfitted for this service. The fact that he probably suspected O'Sullivan of having been responsible for the order may have accounted for Lord George's loss of temper, but it seems hard that the Prince should have had to bear the brunt of it.

For some little time the Camerons who had been posted in the churchyard were undetected, but on one of Cope's volunteers riding up to reconnoitre the Heugh they drew attention to themselves by sniping at him, and Whitefoord was ordered to dislodge them with the artillery. Although mortar-fire would have been more effective than gun-fire, experience had shown that the shells were far from reliable, 'having been long in Store in Edinburgh Castle, prepared, and many of the Fuzes damnified'. It was therefore decided to make use of the cannon, and two of the $1\frac{1}{2}$-pounders were run forward to the edge of the ditch, where they were loaded and fired with the help of the seaman-gunners, some of whom must have been comparatively sober. At each discharge the troops gave a cheer, and although the little round-shot were barely $2\frac{1}{4}$ inches in diameter and the range about 800 yards, the shooting was sufficiently accurate to inflict some casualties. On being informed of them, Lochiel, who saw no purpose in allowing his men to remain exposed, appealed to Lord George Murray for permission to withdraw the party, and he at once agreed. It was not before time, for additional guns were being brought forward to bear on the churchyard.

Murray was by now convinced that the only direction from which to launch a successful attack on the royal army was from the east, and having come to this decision he wasted no time in putting it into effect. Without bothering to consult his fellow-commanders, he ordered Lochiel's regiment to march through Tranent and draw up in the fields to the east of the village, at the same time sending an A.D.C. to the Prince to explain his intentions and request him to follow with the rest of the front-line troops. In deciding to make this movement Lord George was not only influenced by tactical considerations. Among his more valuable qualities as a leader was his understanding of the Highland mind, and knowing that the Highlanders 'had a freit not to turn their backs upon the first sight of the enemy', he realised that it would help to counteract any bad effect resulting from their withdrawal from the churchyard. Lord George himself had no such 'freits', and during the march he was amused to see two further examples of Highland superstition. Shortly before entering the village a hare got up in front of the regiment, and was immediately shot at and killed, much to the terror of a countryman, who thought that he was the target. Later on, while passing through Tranent, a large sow rashly attempted to cross the line of march, and 'in a moment there were twenty dirks in the beast, who fell down dead making such squeaks as may be imagined'.

To O'Sullivan, not probably, in the best of tempers, Lord George's march appeared to be equally ill-advised and ill-executed. While returning from the left for the third time, after giving Lord Nairne the Prince's final instructions with regard to the Athollmen, he had been surprised to see the Highland right in motion. Telling Nairne to do nothing until he had discovered what was happening, O'Sullivan eventually overtook Lord George on his way through Tranent, having been shaken to find that not only had he withdrawn the 50 Camerons and the rest of the out-guards, but was cheerfully committing the military crime of marching in broad daylight with his flank exposed to the enemy. After trying unsuccessfully to persuade him to halt until it became dark and the fields to the east of the village had been reconnoitred, O'Sullivan returned to the left to assist Nairne in posting the Athollmen. He was met on the way by Sir John MacDonald, who found him 'in great distress, because Lord George would do nothing that he advised', and after professional head-shakings over the methods of amateur soldiers, Sir John parted from him, having 'begged him as fervently as I could to work for the service of the Prince and the general cause'.

The movement of the Athollmen on the Jacobite left did not escape notice for long. About 4 o'clock, Carlyle, who had volunteered to keep watch on the enemy from his father's church-tower at Prestonpans, observed a detachment of Highlanders moving westwards down the side of Birsley Brae, a spur of Falside Hill. A little later a larger body, consisting of 300 or 400 men, came into view between Preston and Dolphingstone, and hurriedly descending from the tower, Carlyle rode off to report these movements to the General. Not only had Cope and his staff already seen them, but they had also noticed Lord George's movement on the Highland right, and as it now seemed possible that a simultaneous attack was about to be launched on both flanks of the royal army, Cope changed front from south to south-west, taking up a position slightly to the west of that he had originally occupied. Still keeping his artillery on the left, he ordered the baggage to be moved to the east of Cockenzie.

The westerly movement of the Highland reserve was short-lived, for the unfortunate O'Sullivan had barely returned from posting the troops when they were ordered back to their former position on the ridge above Bankton. Here an advanced-post was set up at a quarry some 250 yards from Bankton House, which during the afternoon had been occupied by a party of the royal troops. As a further precaution against infiltration from that quarter Cope had ordered breaches to be made in the Preston park walls, which had he but known it, were to be put to a very different use.

Cope has been almost universally condemned for having kept his army on the defensive, and if Gardiner's biographer, Dr. Doddridge, is to be believed, the Colonel was among his earliest critics. On the royal army's forming line of battle he had ridden through the ranks of his regiment, calling upon the men 'in the most respectful and animating Manner, both as Soldiers, and as Christians, to . . . engage themselves couragiously in the Service of their Country, and to neglect nothing that might have a Tendency to prepare them for whatever Event might happen'. Despite its slightly sinister tone the troopers were 'much affected' by the Colonel's address, 'and expressed a very ardent Desire of attacking the Enemy immediately; a Desire in which he and another very gallant Officer of distinguished Rank, Dignity, and Character both for Bravery and Conduct, would gladly have gratified them, if it had been in the Power of either'.

Doddridge's statement suggests that he is trying to raise his hero's credit at the expense of the unfortunate Cope, for, if true, it does little to enhance Gardiner's military reputation. Cope had already decided against occupying the enemy's position while he had had the opportunity of doing so, and had he attacked the Highlanders now that they were in possession of it, he would merely have exposed his army to all the disadvantages he had previously foreseen. None of his troops had been in action before, and having had the good fortune to find ground suited for the movement of cavalry, an arm which was virtually absent from the enemy's ranks, and where his infantry could be kept in hand, Cope would rightly have been open to censure had he abandoned it. What seems to have escaped his critics is the fact that he succeeded in making the enemy attack him on his own ground, and that even under such favourable conditions was unable to avoid defeat.

A more sensible suggestion of Gardiner's was that the artillery should be sited in the centre of the line, rather than on one or other of the wings near the cavalry, 'where he was apprehensive, that the Horses, which had not been in any Engagement before, might be thrown into some Disorder by the Discharge so very near them'. There would seem to be no good reason why this suggestion was not adopted, for apart from their effect on the horses, it would have been tactically sounder to have stationed the guns and mortars in the centre. Not only would they have been less isolated, but their fire would have covered a wider front.

By the time that the Atholl Brigade had returned to its former ground it was becoming dark, and Cope ordered the royal army to take up position for the night on a line running parallel to the large ditch, and a little to the east of the one it had occupied earlier in the afternoon. Excepting that the whole of the artillery was posted on the left, the original 'Order of Battle' remained unaltered so far as the front line was concerned, but in the rear the reserve now consisted only of a single squadron belonging to each of the cavalry regiments. This change was the result of Cope's decision to replace the 100 regulars, who had hitherto formed the baggage-guard, by his 180 Highlanders, most of whom were newly-raised and untrained. From his previous experiences he may also have had doubts about their loyalty, and later that evening have felt no great regret as he watched them march off with the baggage and the military chest to an enclosure on the south side of Cockenzie. The volunteers forming the rest of the infantry reserve were still less reliable, and as few of them were properly clad for spending the night in the open, Cope dismissed them with orders to report at dawn the following morning. In doing so he was to save many young lives, for not more than a handful arrived in time to take part in the battle.

In spite of Home's estimate two days earlier that the Highland army numbered under 2,000 men, Cope and his officers had a vastly exaggerated idea of its strength. One of them, who had reconnoitred the Highlanders during their march up Falside Hill, had put it at over 5,000 men, and 'about 5,000' was the estimate of Mr. Baillie, steward to the Solicitor-General, 'who had been in among the Rebels' that evening. Later, at Cope's 'Examination', Whitefoord testified that after being taken prisoner he had been told 'by the Person calling himself the Duke of Perth, and by the Lords George Murray, Elcho, and Nairne, that the number of the Rebels was 5,500'; and two other captured officers, Majors Severn and Talbot, stated that the same figure had been given them by Perth 'by the Returns he had had the Night before the Battle . . .'. Yet the Jacobite leaders must have been well aware that the Highland army's strength was barely half this number. The fact that this absurd over-estimate was accepted as correct by Cope and his officers is less surprising in the light of certain incidents which occurred during the action.

In face of these supposed odds, and despite his strong defensive position, Cope was determined not to be taken by surprise, and no fewer than 200 dragoons and 300 infantry were detailed as out-guards. Of these, 100 dragoons under a Captain and two subalterns were posted to guard the narrow defile between Bankton and Preston House, and on the left the same number was stationed to cover the approaches from Seton and the east end of the morass. In support of the dragoons strong infantry guards were posted well in advance of the line, and two platoons were later ordered to assist in guarding the southern defile at the back of Preston House. In rear, the other western route, between Preston park walls and Preston-pans, was protected by Gardiner's reserve squadron, while that of Hamilton's covered the eastern approaches between Seton and the sea. As an additional precaution against surprise three large fires were lit along the front of the line.

The night was dark and cold, with an autumnal nip in the air, but on visiting Colonel Gardiner for the last time Carlyle found him bivouacking with his regiment on the right of the line. He was 'grave, but serene and resigned; and he concluded by praying God to bless me, and that he could not wish for a better night to lie on the field; and then called for his cloak and other conveniences for lying down, as he said they would be awaked early enough in the morning, as he thought, by the countenance of the enemy . . .'. Among the other calumnies with which Cope has been loaded is the assertion that, in contrast to Gardiner, he spent the night in a house in Cockenzie. Such a statement shows a remarkable lack of insight into Cope's character, for so anxious-minded a man would have been the last to put his personal comfort before his duty. In any case Captain Forbes of Read's (9th) Foot, who was serving as a volunteer sets the matter beyond all doubt, for in his account of the battle he mentions that 'every half hour the General who continu'd in the Line received the Reports of the Patroles'.

By now Cope had little hope of being joined by the gunners from Edinburgh Castle, although one faint chance remainéd. During the afternoon Lieut. Craig, of Wynyard's (17th) Foot, and like Forbes a volunteer, had offered to carry a final message to Guest, requesting the services of 'the chief engineer' and some of the gunners. On arriving at the Castle at 11 o'clock that night Craig found the old general in a far from helpful mood. He asserted that he was unable to spare the chief engineer, but 'after making some Difficulties' detailed a bombardier and four gunners. Craig, who was well-known to some of the Jacobite leaders, 'who would not fail of suspecting his Business', considered it safer not to accompany them. Instead, having disguised them 'like Tradesmen', he sent them off under the guidance of a countryman, but, due either to the man's stupidity or political views, the party failed to reach the royal army. Even without their help Cope had hoped to 'annoy' the enemy by shelling their position during the night, but he was forced to abandon this plan after a single round fired from one of the mortars had raised doubts. Once again the 'damnified fuzes' had been found wanting.

During the earlier part of the evening all remained quiet, but about 8 o'clock there was 'a pretty smart Firing' near Bankton House where one of Cope's dragoon patrols was attacked by men of the Highland reserve, and shortly afterwards the Highland front line began moving eastwards to join Lochiel's regiment on the other side of Tranent. This movement was a far from silent one, for about 9 o'clock 'all the Dogs in the Village ... began to bark with the utmost Fury', and their barking continued for the next hour and a half. It was correctly interpreted by Cope and his staff as indicating a large-scale change of position, although the retention of the Highland reserve to the west of the village made its object uncertain.

On completion of this movement the Jacobite leaders met to discuss the final arrangements for attacking the royal army at day-break, and Lord George Murray outlined his plan. Bold yet simple, it consisted of marching round the east end of the morass and falling on the enemy's open flank. He wrote:

'I told them I knew the ground myself and had a gentleman or two with me who knew every part thereabouts; there was, indeed, a small defile at the east end of the ditches; but once that was past, there would be no stop, and though we should be long on our march, yet when the whole line was past the defile, they had nothing to do but face left, and in a moment the whole was formed, and then to attack.'

According to Lord George, the Prince and the other officers— O'Sullivan was with the reserve—were 'highly pleased' with his plan, and after the meeting was over and out-guards had been posted the army settled down for the rest of the night.

The field it occupied had been under pease, recently cut, and using the straw as bedding the officers and men lay down in rank and file, in order to be ready to march at short notice. For supper they ate whatever food they had managed to bring with them, and the Prince, in high spirits, and forgetting his unfortunate brush with Lord George, was 'great at Cup & Can' with him.

During the meeting of the Jacobite leaders, Robert Anderson, the son of a local laird, had sat silent. He had been too modest to take part in the discussion of Lord George's plan of attack, but afterwards sought out his friend, Colonel Hepburn of Keith, and told him that he knew of a much less roundabout approach to the royal army's position. He had often made use of this track when snipe-shooting in the morass, its chief disadvantage being that at one point it passed through a narrow defile, which could be easily guarded by the enemy. Hepburn was much impressed by Anderson's suggestion, and advised him to put it before Lord George Murray, adding, with considerable insight, that his lordship would take it better from Anderson himself than through an intermediary. Acting on Hepburn's advice, Anderson awakened Lord George, who was equally impressed by his suggestion, as were the Prince and the rest of the officers, and orders were sent to Lord Nairne to march at 2 a.m. and rejoin the Highland main body.

It seems strange that there is not the slightest reference to Anderson's intervention in Lord George's *Marches of the Highland Army* beyond the following not entirely accurate statement: 'At midnight the principal officers were called again, and all was ordered as was at first proposed.' Why, then, it may be asked, should it have been necessary to hold a second meeting?

Nairne and his men arrived in good time, and shortly before 4 a.m.

the Highland army began its march. Having brought up the rear of
the front-line troops the previous day, it was now the turn of the
MacDonalds to take the van, and led by Clanranald's regiment the
first column moved off from the left. Following Clanranald's were
Glengarry's and Keppoch's regiments, including the MacDonalds
of Glencoe; Perth's men and the MacGregors; and in rear, the
Stewarts of Appin and Lochiel's Camerons. By virtue of seniority
the van, or right of the line, was commanded by the Duke of Perth,
and the rear, or left, by Lord George Murray. Closely following the
front-line troops was the reserve under the Prince and Lord Nairne,
consisting, in order of march, of the two regiments forming the
Atholl Brigade, and the MacLachlans. Silence was essential, and for
this reason Lord Strathallan's troopers were ordered to remain in
rear until the infantry had passed the defile, and all officers were
required to fight on foot lest the movement of their horses should
betray the army's approach.

Guided by Anderson, and moving very slowly north-eastwards
down the ridge, the head of the leading column passed safely through
the narrow defile close to the farm of Riggonhead. So far there had
been no sound or movement on the part of the enemy, but shortly
before Anderson was about to lead the way through the morass
there was a shout of 'Who's there?' from a party of patrolling
dragoons. No answer was returned, but the troopers' suspicions
were aroused, and they galloped off to raise the alarm. By this time
dawn was beginning to break, and a cold morning mist hung low
over the marshland as the shadowy column wound its way forward
in almost complete silence. Here, at its eastern end, the morass was
bounded on the north by nothing more formidable than a four-foot
ditch, and having crossed it by a narrow plank bridge the Highland
vanguard entered the plain about 1,000 yards to the east of the royal
army's left flank.

Continuing in a northerly direction towards Cockenzie, the head
of the column marched on until it was estimated that the rear of the
front-line troops had got clear of the marsh, but in the half-light this
was largely a matter of guesswork, and anxious to be on the safe side,
Perth carried on for too long a distance. In consequence, when he
eventually halted and turned left to form line, the rear, which had
already done so, became separated from his wing by a gap until
just before the Highland attack began. It may have been their failure

to observe this gap, combined with the outflanking of the royal army's left wing, that made Cope and his officers all the more ready to accept the over-estimate of the Highland army's strength.*

Meanwhile the reserve had still to make its way through the marsh, and Lord George sent off Johnstone to see that it did so without noise or confusion. All went well, but to cross the ditch the Prince attempted to leap over it, and fell forward on to his knees on the muddy far bank. Taking him by the arm Johnstone helped him to his feet, and from the expression on the Prince's face it seemed to him that Charles considered the accident a bad omen.

On reaching the plain the reserve drew up some 50 yards in rear of the front line, and to safeguard his flank Lord George Murray gave orders for one of the three reserve regiments to move up between the Camerons and the marsh. Owing, however, to the distance his A.D.C. had to cover on foot, and the short interval of time before the attack began, these orders failed to arrive.

One point to which Cope attached particular importance was the fact that at the beginning of the action his army was fully formed. That this was true there can be no doubt, not only from the statements of eye-witnesses on both sides but from the inferences to be drawn from certain incidents. From 3 o'clock onwards, when his patrols first reported the eastward movement of the Highland reserve, Cope had been aware that something was in the wind, and on receiving the dragoons' report of the threat to his left wing he at once ordered one of the 1½-pounders to be fired as an alarm gun to recall the out-guards. According to Elcho this signal was heard just as the reserve was passing through the defile at the Riggonhead farm, while Johnstone, who was with the Prince, says that the reserve was 'not yet out of the marsh, when the enemy, seeing our first line in order of battle, fired an alarm gun'. Though not fully in agreement both at any rate make it clear that, at the time the royal

* Whitefoord estimated the length of the royal army front line (including intervals) as 669 paces, and 100 paces as the distance it was outflanked on the left by the Highland army. On this basis he calculated that the Highland front line 'without any interval in their line as is proved by many Officers and Country Gentlemen', numbered 3,450 men. To this figure he added 2,000 as the strength of the Highland reserve, making a total of 5,450 men. Vide *The Whitefoord Papers*, p. 58.

army received the alarm, the Highland reserve had anything up to half a mile to march before reaching its battle position—much the same distance, in fact, as that to be covered by the royal army in taking up its own. As for Johnstone's statement that by this time the Highland front line was already formed, this can only have been true of the left wing; as will soon be seen, the right wing was then still on the march.

Having called in his out-guards, Cope immediately ordered the royal army to face the enemy. To do so as rapidly as possible, the infantry was wheeled to the left by platoons, and led by Major Talbot of Murray's, the Field-Officer of the Day, it marched off in a northerly direction, roughly parallel to the line of march of the Highlanders. It was now becoming lighter, and from his position at the head of the column Talbot caught sight of the enemy 'extending their Line towards the Sea', thus disproving Johnstone's statement that the Highland front line was fully formed.

On halting and turning right into line, the royal infantry, three deep, faced east, with its left towards Cockenzie, and its right protected by the large ditch. Drawn up from left to right were 9 companies of Murray's, 8 of Lascelles's, 2 of Guise's, and 5 of Lee's. To the right of Lee's companies, and separated from them by an interval sufficient to leave room for two squadrons of cavalry, was the artillery. With the guns on the left, and the mortars on their right, it was dressed in line with the infantry, with 6-feet intervals between the pieces. Immediately to the right of the mortars was posted an artillery guard of 100 men, most of whom belonged to Capt. Cochran's company of Murray's regiment.

Meanwhile the dragoons had been ordered to mount, and riding up to the front of Gardiner's regiment Brigadier Fowke called out: 'My lads, this is the Day, in which I doubt not, your Behaviour will do us Honour.' He was soon to be disillusioned. To take full advantage of his cavalry superiority, Cope had ordered the squadrons to form two-deep instead of the customary three-deep, and having left a squadron of each regiment in reserve, the remaining two squadrons of Gardiner's and Hamilton's moved up to take position in the line. Hamilton's on the extreme left had no difficulty in doing so, but on the right it was found that there was insufficient room between Lee's and the artillery for Colonel Gardiner's and Lieut.-Colonel Whitney's squadrons. This was due to the return of the 300 infantry out-guards, who having too little time to rejoin their respective regiments, had been fallen-in as they arrived to the right of Lee's companies. In consequence, Fowke ordered Gardiner's squadron to fall back in rear of the artillery. There is no explanation of the Colonel's demotion from the command of the left wing to that of a single squadron, and it can only be assumed that since issuing the 'Order of Battle' at Haddington, Cope had realised his unfitness for the post.

As the troops took up their positions Cope rode along the front of the line from right to left, 'Encouraging the Men, begging them to keep up their Fire, & keep their Ranks, & they would Easily beat the Rebells'. On arriving at the left he was annoyed to find that Hamilton's squadrons had not yet drawn swords, and ordered them immediately to do so. Almost at the same moment the Highland front line began to advance, and observing that his left wing was considerably outflanked, Cope despatched his senior A.D.C., Major Mossman, with orders to Lieut.-Colonel Whitefoord, to send over two guns from the right. Mossman arrived too late, for seized by panic, the civilian drivers had ridden off with the train-horses, closely followed by the seaman-gunners.

The sun had barely risen when the Highland army began its attack. Separated by the wide gap, it was difficult to synchronise the movements of the wings, but without waiting for instructions from Perth, Lord George Murray ordered the left wing to advance. His A.D.C., sent to inform the Duke, was met by young Anderson with a message from Perth, saying he was ready to go forward. In consequence, although soon afterwards followed by the right, the Highland left thus gained a considerable lead.

Seeing that the Camerons were in some danger of being outflanked, Lord George had advised Lochiel that his men should incline towards the left as they advanced. It was therefore from this direction that their attack was directed on the royal right. Their plaids discarded, and with their bonnets pulled low over their brows, the Highlanders came on with 'a hideous shout'. Terrified, the old gunner and the three invalids turned and fled, and left, single-handed, to manage the artillery, Whitefoord and Griffith opened fire. Taking aim as best they could, Whitefoord succeeded in discharging five of the $1\frac{1}{2}$-pounders, and Griffith all six of the mortars, though how many of the defective shells burst it was impossible to observe. Nevertheless their fire produced some effect, for the enemy line was seen to give 'a great Shake', at which the royal troops 'huzza'd'. They were still in good heart, and had the artillery been manned by regular gunners its effect might have been decisive.

Recovering almost at once, the Highlanders returned the cheer, and broke up into several separate bodies, of which three on their left wing advanced 'with a swiftness not to be conceived', firing as they came. The largest of them, which consisted of Lochiel's men, 'at least 20 in Front, and 30 in Depth', made straight for the artillery, and Whitefoord, seeing them to be in some confusion, called out to Whitney that now was his time to attack. At almost the same moment Whitney received orders from Lord Loudon to charge the Highlanders in the flank, and leading his squadron out of the line 'very gallantly', he managed to get within pistol-shot of them. His example was of no avail, for after receiving four or five musket-shots his men refused to follow him, 'and immediately the Rear Rank began to run away, and the rest followed in Tens and Twenties'. Whitney himself was shot through the sword-arm.

Meanwhile the infantry had begun to show signs of unsteadiness. Not only had the artillery-guard left its ground and crowded in a confused mass behind the guns and mortars, but when instructed by Colonel Lascelles to wheel in support of Whitney's squadron, some of the platoons on the right of the line were seen to be 'crouching and creeping gently backwards, with their Arms recovered', and the order had to be countermanded.

Gardiner's squadron, too, had not been slow to take alarm. His men 'began to be a little shy' when they saw the artillery-guard fall back in disorder, whereupon Fowke shouted angrily to them: 'What do you mean, Gentlemen, by reining back your Horses? Advance up to your Ground; have you anything to fear? We shall cut them to Pieces in a Moment.' He ordered Gardiner to incline his squadron to the left so as to give it more room to advance, and then, with his Brigade-Major, Captain Singleton, tried to reorganise the artillery-guard. An irregular front rank was formed with the help of some of the sergeants, but it gave way as soon as it had delivered 'a straggling fire', and both artillery and artillery-guard were over-run by the oncoming Highlanders. Seeing that they had lost all semblance of formation, and were in a state of confusion, Loudon ordered Gardiner to charge, but having received a few shots which killed or

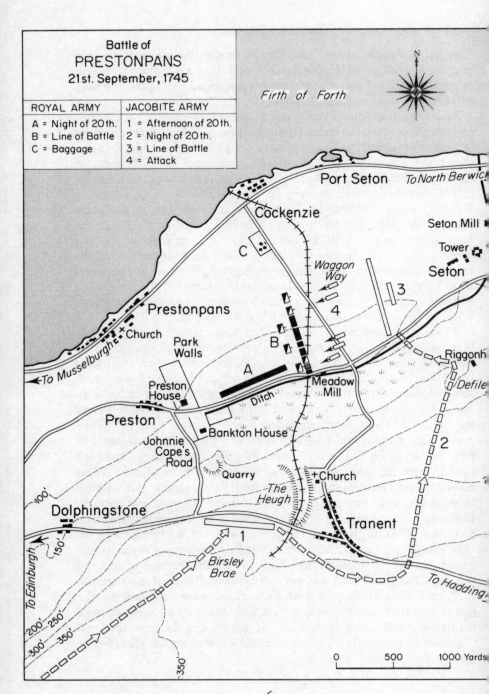

Battle of
PRESTONPANS
21st. September, 1745

ROYAL ARMY	JACOBITE ARMY
A = Night of 20th.	1 = Afternoon of 20th.
B = Line of Battle	2 = Night of 20th.
C = Baggage	3 = Line of Battle
	4 = Attack

N

Firth of Forth

Port Seton   To North Berwick

Cockenzie

Seton Mill

Tower

C   Seton

Waggon
Way

Prestonpans   3

4

Church

Park
Walls   B   Riggonh

A   Defile

To Musselburgh   Meadow
Mill

Preston
House   Ditch

Preston   Bankton House

Johnnie
Cope's
Road   2

Quarry

Church

The
Heugh

Dolphingstone   Tranent

To Edinburgh   150'   1   To Hadding.

Birsley
Brae

100'

200' 250'

300'

350'

350'

0   500   1000 Yards

wounded some of the horses, his squadron, with the exception of about 15 men, turned tail and fled. His gloomy forecast had been all-too accurate.

Matters were no better at the other end of the line, where, armed only with a riding-whip, the intrepid Lord Drummore had stationed himself on the flank, 'resolved to see the Fate of a Battle in which I was most sensibly interested'. Mounted on horseback about 150 yards to the left of Hamilton's squadrons, he had an excellent view of the royal left on which he saw the Highlanders advancing in 'two Columns, Clews, or Clumps ... and upon the Right of those Columns a long Line which far outflank'd our Line'. From his description it is clear that although, like the Camerons and Stewarts on the Highland left wing, some of the MacDonalds broke up into separate bodies, those on the extreme right managed to preserve their line formation. In fact, so orderly was it, that while they were advancing Drummore 'could see thro' from Front to Rear, yet to my Astonishment, every Front Man cover'd his Followers, there was no Man to be seen in the Open ... in short, tho' their Motion was very quick, it was uniform and orderly, and I confess I was surprized at it'.

Since, as Drummore mentions, the Highland right greatly outflanked the royal left, the attack, like that on the opposite wing, was in an oblique direction. Swinging in towards the royal army's left flank, the MacDonalds fired some 'dropping Shot' at long range, which killed or wounded several men and horses of Hamilton's squadrons, but the dragoons did not await their coming. Seized by the same panic that had afflicted Gardiner's men, they galloped off 'not in a Body, but quite broke in two's or so', following hard on the heels of the reserve squadron which was already on its way to the rear.

Deserted by the cavalry, the unfortunate infantry now faced the full fury of the Highlanders' attack. Most of Lochiel's men had already gone in pursuit of the flying dragoons, 'Sword in Hand as fast as they could run'. About 150 of them, however, halted on the right of the artillery to await the arrival of the other two columns, and when these had come up they fell upon the royalist right. Colonel Lascelles tried to form a flank against them by ordering the wing platoons to wheel outwards, but his men refused to stand their ground. While directing this movement he fell, and on getting to his feet was confronted by a Highland officer with a party of 16 men, who told him he was a prisoner. They ordered him to give up his arms, but immediately rushed on in pursuit, and the Colonel was able to make his way between the oncoming columns to escape to Seton.

At the beginning of the action Cope had ridden over to the right, but by the time he reached it the dragoons had already given way. Returning towards the left, he now tried with the rest of the officers to get the foot to stand fast and make a regular fire. But entreaties and threats were alike useless, and after giving what Drummore described as an 'infamous' fire, the infantry was broken into from right to left by successive waves of Highlanders. Throwing down their muskets, they seized broadsword and dirk, and closing in on the terror-stricken redcoats, they hacked and stabbed their way forward among what soon became a flying rabble with no thought but of escape. Far from behaving like the coward of popular tradition Cope rode in among the broken foot, calling upon them to halt, and Captain Pointz of Guise's heard him shout to them: 'For Shame, Gentlemen, behave like Britons, give them another Fire, and you'll make them run', and Lieutenant Greenwell of Murray's: 'For Shame, Gentlemen, don't let us be beat by such a Set of Banditti.'

Finding it impossible to rally the foot, Cope, joined by Lords Loudon and Home, next tried to round up the dragoons. Most of Gardiner's troopers had made for the narrow defile south of Preston House, which soon became choked by a mob of shouting, swearing men and terrified horses, all struggling desperately to force their way through. Others with their horses' croups turned to the enemy huddled together under the park walls, or dismounting, crawled through the breaches made in them the previous afternoon, while many of Hamilton's men escaped to Prestonpans. As it was equally impossible to get the dragoons to make a stand, and since most of them had by this time forced their way through the defile, Cope rode through them, intending to bring them to a halt on the far side. At the west end of Preston village he met Lord Home, pistol in hand, turning the runaways into a field, and with the help of Lord Loudon and some of the dragoon officers about 450 of them were got together. A squadron was formed, and shortly afterwards, on a body of Highlanders appearing at the other end of the village, it was ordered to attack them, 'seeing they stood in Awe'. So also did the dragoons, who could not be prevailed upon 'to move one Foot', and realising that it was hopeless to expect anything further of them, Cope and the rest of the officers rode off at their head, as this was found to be the only way of keeping them together. The lane along which they retreated from Preston up the side of Birsley Brae, is still known as 'Johnnie Cope's Road'.

In spite of having posted himself with his life-guards well in advance of the Highland reserve, the Prince saw little of the fighting. Scarcely more than five minutes elapsed from the onslaught on the royal foot to the breaking of the entire front line, and by the time that he and the reserve came up 'we saw no other enemy on the field of battle', wrote Johnstone, 'than those who were lying on the ground killed and wounded, though we were not more than fifty paces behind our first line, running always as fast as we could to overtake them, and near enough never to lose sight of them'.

In the rout that followed, the royal infantry, encumbered by their tight clothing and heavier equipment, had little chance of escape. In their panic they threw away their arms in order to run faster, and following the dragoons' example fled back to the park walls of Preston, where some few managed to find their way to safety through the breaches, but many more were killed as they tried to climb the high walls, or struggled to reach the defile. Few fell by small-arm fire; nearly all by the broadsword, and the battlefield 'presented a spectacle of horror, being covered with heads, legs, and arms, and mutilated bodies . . . '. It was indeed a formidable weapon, and a single stroke of a Highland officer's sword is said to have severed the arm of a grenadier of Murray's raised to ward off the blow, and to have penetrated his skull, so that he died instantly. Hardly less effective were the scythe-blades of a company of MacGregors belonging to the Duke of Perth's regiment, which 'cut the legs of the horses in two; and their riders through the middle of their bodies', and as a historian has remarked, the sight of such butchery must have had the same effect on many of the young soldiers as it was to have a century later on those who fought in the Zulu wars. Nor would their stories of bloodshed and terror lose anything in the telling, and as fear breeds cruelty, it is not over-fanciful to suppose that some of the royal army's excesses after Culloden were inspired by them.

The Highlander, once his blood is up, is not remarkable for self-control, and Lord George Murray's statement that 'never was quarter given with more humanity than by the Highlanders', is difficult to reconcile with the fact that immediately the rout began, the Duke of Perth and the other Jacobite leaders mounted and rode about the field, calling on their men to spare the officers. Among them were Lieut.-Colonel Peter Halkett of Lee's, and a small party of officers and men, who were firing on the Camerons from the far side of the ditch. Seeing a hundred Highlanders about to retaliate, Lord George persuaded the party to surrender, 'and nothing', he afterwards wrote, 'gave me more pleasure that day, than having it so immediately in my power to save these men, as well as several others'. Halkett, with equal honour, was afterwards one of the few officers who refused to break his parole.

Soon after this incident Lord Elcho, who with some of the better-mounted of Lord Strathallan's men, had pressed on behind the Highland infantry, reported to Lord George and Lochiel that a small body of what appeared to be the enemy was gathering on the ridge beside Tranent. Ordering the pipes to be played, Lochiel quickly called in his men and with Lord George marched up the slope towards the village, only to find when half-way there that the 'enemy' were country people and servants belonging to the Highland army. Almost simultaneously a message arrived from the Prince to say that Cope's baggage-guard was still holding out at Cockenzie, and turning about, the Camerons marched off to attack it. On arriving at the village Lord George, again seeking to avoid bloodshed, sent Halkett with a summons to surrender, and seeing that further resistance was useless, the Highland companies laid down their arms. Apart from the baggage, another valuable capture was Cope's papers and his military chest, containing between two and three thousand pounds, which were found hidden under a stair in Cockenzie House.

Even before the action was over the Highlanders had begun plundering the dead. Arms, ammunition, musket-locks, clothing, money, valuables of all kinds, were eagerly seized upon, and there is the well-known story of the Highlander who parted with a watch for next to nothing, remarking that 'he was glad to be rid of the creature, for she lived no time after he caught her'—the works having run down.

A lifelike though partisan portrait of the Prince on the morning of victory is drawn by Andrew Henderson, the Whig historian:

'. . . I went to the Road-Side where the Chevalier, who by Advice of Perth, &c. had sent to Edinburgh for Surgeons, was standing. He was clad as an ordinary Captain, in a coarse Plaid and blue Bonnet, his Boots and Knees were much dirtied; he seemed to have fallen into a Ditch, which I was told by one of his Lifeguards he had. He was exceeding merry: Speaking of his Army, he said twice, "My High-landmen have lost their Plaids." At which he laughed very heartily. When talking of the Wounded, he seemed no Way affected. There were seven Standards taken, which when he saw, he said in French, a Language he frequently spoke in, "We have missed some of them." Then he refreshed himself upon the Field and with the utmost Composure eat a Piece of cold Beef, and drank a Glass of Wine, amidst the deep and piercing Groans of the wounded and dying, who had fallen a Sacrifice to his Ambition.'

Henderson's tribute to the Duke of Perth was well deserved, for he and Lord George Murray did their best to see that the wounded on both sides were properly cared for. Most of the badly wounded Highlanders were taken to Bankton House, which was turned into a hospital, although this did not save it from being plundered 'to the very Curtains of the Beds, and Hangings of the Rooms'. At Preston-pans, where two of the dragoon surgeons were attending to the wounded officers of the royal army, Carlyle saw a young man, Captain Blake, who had had a piece of his skull shorn off by a broadsword. Although apparently dying, his skull was skilfully trepanned, and 55 years later he sent Carlyle an invitation to visit him in London. In contrast to the Jacobites' humanity some of the local inhabitants seem to have shown the utmost callousness. For when walking over the battlefield in the afternoon Lord George saw a few of the worst-wounded of Cope's men still lying there, 'and though there were several of the country people of that neighbour-hood looking at them, I could not prevail with them to carry them to houses, but got some of our people to do it'.

Nearly 80 of the royal army officers were taken prisoner, many of them wounded, but thanks to the intervention of the Jacobite leaders no more than seven were killed. Among them was Colonel Gardiner, whose end is dramatically described by Dr. Doddridge. Shot in the left breast at the beginning of the action, and soon after-wards in the right thigh, the Colonel stood his ground after his squadron had fled, and seeing a party of foot still fighting without an officer to lead them, he rode up and called out to them, 'Fire on, my Lads, and fear nothing.' A moment later he received a deep wound in the right arm from a scythe-blade, and having been dragged from his horse, was struck a mortal blow on the back of his head by a Highlander with a Lochaber axe. Taking up his hat in his left hand the Colonel waved it to his servant as a signal to retreat, with the words, 'Take care of yourself.' On returning two hours later with a cart, the man found that Gardiner had been stripped of his outer clothing and boots, and robbed of his watch and other valuables, and having been carried in a semi-conscious condition to the manse of Tranent, he died there the following morning. That Gardiner fought bravely there can be no doubt, but Doddridge's narrative, which was given him by the Colonel's servant, is almost certainly untrue. Apart from the improbability of a man in his state of health being able to retain his powers of movement and speech after being so severely wounded, the evidence of his relative Cornet Ker, who was posted 'very near' him, seems conclusive. According to him the Colonel fell from his horse after receiving two gun-shot wounds in the right side. Having no servant or spare horse in attendance he was unable to remount, and almost immediately afterwards was brought to the ground by six cuts in the head. Ker added that Gardiner's wounds had been 'certify'd' to him by the surgeon who had attended the Colonel, the minister of Tranent, and Gardiner's 'body servant'.

On the Jacobite side six officers were killed, of whom the most noteworthy were young David Threipland of Fingask, and Malcolm MacGregor, who commanded one of Perth's companies. Attended only by two servants, Threipland had pursued a party of dragoons, who suddenly turned and shot him dead. He was buried where he fell, and years afterwards Scott remembered, as a child, sitting on his grave. MacGregor, whom Johnstone describes as 'whimsical and singular', was hit in five places, and after he was wounded called out to his men, 'My lads, I am not dead, and, by God, I shall see if any of you does not do his duty.' He died soon after the battle.

The casualties among the rank and file of the royal army are difficult to assess, for no official Government figures appear to have been issued, and those available are nearly all derived from Jacobite sources. Under the heading of 'Killed' the numbers range from Johnstone's ridiculous figure of 1,300 to Murray of Broughton's more modest total of 300, while Home puts the figure as low as 200, and the official Jacobite communiqué at 500. Of these, Broughton's estimate is probably the most accurate. Under 'Wounded' his figure of between 400 and 500 would also seem to be much nearer the truth than the 'official' Jacobite figure of 900. On the number of prisoners there is more agreement, although Lord George Murray's total of between 1,600 and 1,700, which was compiled from lists made by the N.C.O's. of the royal regiments, is rather higher than the rest. These vary between 1,400 and 1,500, and confirm Home's statement that of the survivors, all except 170 of the infantry were captured, although many afterwards succeeded in making their escape.

The 'official' Jacobite casualties of 30 killed and between 70 and 80 wounded have been questioned as unduly high, and it has been suggested that they were purposely magnified in order to lend colour to the Jacobite account of the battle. This is not unlikely, for its writer who speaks of the 'very regular fire of the dragoons on the right and left' and the 'close platoons of all their infantry' was certainly given to exaggeration.

A 'return' of Hamilton's shows that the regiment 'lost' 87 horses at Prestonpans, and the figure for Gardiner's was probably much the same. Whether they were captured or killed is less easy to say, for Elcho makes the curious comment that 'their would have been a great many more taken, had it not been for a notion the Highlanders had that the horses fought as well as the men, which made them kill a great many of them after their riders were dismounted'.

To the captured officers their defeat was nothing short of a disgrace, and Carlyle, who saw them walking on the shore near Prestonpans, describes the expression on their faces as being a mixture of shame, dejection, and despair. 'They were deeply mortified with what had happened, and timidly anxious about the future, for they were doubtful whether they were to be treated as prisoners of war or as rebels.' They had little cause for anxiety, for in addition to finding them quarters and supplying them with food and liquor of his own, Lord George Murray spent the night in their company in case they should be molested by drunken Highlanders. The men were similarly provided for, and Lord George arranged for a supply of their own army biscuit to be brought from Cockenzie to the courts and gardens of Bankton where they were confined for the night.

Fowke and Lascelles were more fortunate. After attempting to rally Gardiner's squadrons during their flight to Preston park walls,

Fowke had galloped back to the right, only to find that the royal foot had already broken. Narrowly avoiding capture, he rode off towards the sea and arrived at Berwick the same night, where he had the presence of mind to send out boats to warn the commander of the Dutch regiment against landing in the Firth of Forth. From Seton, Lascelles also succeeded in escaping to Berwick, where later, much to the annoyance of Lieut.-Colonel Whitney, he heaped 'a Profusion of Reproaches' on the conduct of the dragoons. In a letter denying Lascelles's allegations, Whitney suggested that the Colonel's own retreat had been hardly less rapid, for 'the Action ending at Half an Hour after 5 o'clock, you was seen at the Post House at Haddington At half an Hour after 6, Eight long scotch Miles from the Field of Battle'. 'I can now', he ended, 'no more allow myself to think I am in any Shape, Your Humble Servant, Shugbrough Whitney.'

Marching south by Lauder, Cope and the dragoons reached Coldstream on the night of the battle, and arrived at Berwick the following afternoon, where Lord Mark Kerr is said to have greeted him with the sarcastic comment that he was the first general to bring the news of his own defeat. It is a pity to spoil a good story, but, in fact, a report of the action had reached Berwick before noon the previous day, and Lord Mark wrote that at his meeting with Cope 'nothing passed'. There was, however, some argument between them as to whether Cope's troops, now on English soil, still remained under Sir John's command, and to avoid further bickering Lord Mark left Berwick. Before doing so he was unable to resist a spiteful parting shot: 'I said, God bless you, Gentlemen, I go to morrow; things have been conducted very well hitherto, I wish you may henceforward conduct matters as they ought to be for his Majesties Service.'

When asked at his subsequent 'Examination' before a Board of General Officers 'from what Cause he imagined, or conceived, the shameful and scandalous Behaviour of the Soldiers proceeded', Cope replied that he knew of no other reason than that they were seized by 'a sudden Pannick'. On what had led to their panic he was silent, but in his despatch to Tweeddale written on the day of the action, he gave as a possible explanation 'the Manner in which the Enemy came on, which was quicker than can be described . . .'. There is little doubt that he was right, for the speed of the Highlanders' attack was entirely at variance with the slow and decorous movements to which his men were accustomed. They had, in fact, been given a lesson in the art of irregular warfare, and ten years later, under Braddock in North America, Lee's, then commanded by the gallant Halkett, was to receive a still harsher one.

At the same time there is also no doubt that Cope's troops—particularly the dragoons—were not only inexperienced but ill-disciplined, and a contributory cause of his defeat was the lack of training of the dragoon horses. For, as Fortescue observes, little attempt was made in those days to accustom them to fire-arms, and he instances the fact that at Dettingen both the King's and Cumberland's chargers took fright and bolted.

Despite the verdict of the Board that Cope 'did his Duty as an Officer, both before, at, and after the Action: And that his personal Behaviour was without Reproach', it is difficult to acquit him of a distinctly casual attitude with regard to his artillery. For in spite of Forbes's warning early in July, it was not until 3rd August, when acknowledging Tweeddale's report of the Prince's landing, that he remarked *en passant*: 'If I come to want to make Use of any Field Train or Artillery at all, we have not any Gunners for that Purpose.' Cope's delay in mentioning this important fact and his doubt about whether to employ artillery are equally surprising. For even if, as Scott suggests, the Highlanders had lost much of their former dread of 'the musket's mother', a well-manned train would have greatly increased his army's morale, and what could be done with one in expert hands was to be demonstrated by Cumberland at Culloden.

To the Government the news of Prestonpans came as a severe shock. Soon after the outbreak of the Rising 6,000 Dutch troops had been ordered to Britain under the terms of a former treaty, and had not part landed 'providentially the day before the news of Cope's defeat', wrote the Duke of Newcastle to Cumberland, 'the confusion in the City of London would not have been to be described, and the King's crown, I will venture to say, in the utmost danger'. They were followed two days after the battle by 10 British battalions, earlier recalled from Flanders, and orders were now sent recalling still more troops.

These and other measures taken by the Government received widespread public support, and all over England 'loyal associations' sprang up pledging men and money in defence of the establishment.

Letters, speeches, and sermons poured from the press, denouncing the claims of the Popish pretender, and painting lurid pictures of what might be expected under his rule. In the London theatres the national anthem was sung with an additional verse reflecting the feelings of the day:

> *From France and pretender*
> *Great Britain defend her,*
>   *Foes let them fall:*
> *From foreign slavery,*
> *Priests and their knavery,*
> *And Popish reverie,*
>   *God save us all.*

Although in retrospect it is obvious that much of this patriotic fervour was whipped up by skilful Whig propaganda, underlying it all was the Englishman's deep-rooted aversion to Roman Catholicism, and his inherent respect for law and order. Or, as one writer succinctly puts it: 'Hanover might be hated, but Papacy and rebellion were hated vastly more.'

In Scotland the outward result of the Prince's victory was that excepting for the castles of Edinburgh, Stirling, and Dumbarton, and the Highland forts and barracks, the whole of the country was in Jacobite hands. Morally, its effect was still more far-reaching, for on paper, at least, a well-equipped regular army had been routed in less than ten minutes by a collection of raw Highland levies. On waverers, such as the wily Lord Lovat, its influence was decisive, and declaring it to be 'the greatest victory that had ever been gained', he ordered his eldest son to lead out the Frasers. To the French, the battle, and the resultant withdrawal of the British troops from Flanders, suggested that what had seemed a forlorn hope might turn out to be a profitable side-show.

In Charles's mind Prestonpans implanted the fatal belief that his Highlanders were invincible.

4

Into England

HAVING SPENT the night of the battle at Pinkie House, the Prince returned with his army next day to Edinburgh. By his express orders no public celebrations were held to mark his victory, for 'he was far from rejoicing att the death of any of his father's subjects, tho never so much his Enemys . . .'. It was at first suggested that, to reap the full advantage of his success, the Prince should march immediately on Berwick, but this plan was soon discarded on account of his shortage of numbers. Instead, it was decided to build up the strength of the Highland army, and for nearly six weeks it remained at Edinburgh.

For over a week after the battle, communications between town and Castle were allowed to remain uninterrupted, but having heard that the garrison was short of provisions, the Prince determined to 'streten' it still further by cutting off its daily supplies. In reply, Guest opened fire with the Castle guns, and during the next five days the garrison made a series of sorties under cover of their shot. During these operations some houses were demolished and set on fire, and 'those who lived exposed to the Castle, removed; and carried out the aged and infirm at the imminent hazard of their lives. . . . It was a very affecting Scene.' Jacobite casualties were small, but several civilians were killed and wounded, and realising that the popularity of his cause was becoming endangered, the Prince called off the blockade.

Time was of vital importance, and urgent appeals were issued calling for reinforcements. Lovat, still trying to keep up appearances with Lord President Forbes, was evasive, unlike the Skye chieftains, MacLeod and Sir Alexander MacDonald, who by now had decided to support the Government. The loyalties of the Mackenzies,

Mackintoshes, Gordons, and Grants were divided; while, as on former occasions, the most northerly clans—Mackays, Sutherlands and Munros—were solidly against the Stuarts. Above all, there was the persuasive influence of the Lord President with which to contend. For having been given a free hand to raise 20 'independent companies' of Highlanders for Government service, he was using the offer of a company as a bait to waverers. This 'intirely putt a Stop to most of these Gentlemens balancing, as a Great Many that the Prince Counted upon accepted of them'.

Yet in spite of such discouragements, and the prevalence of desertion, especially among the Athollmen, the Highland army's numbers slowly increased. Young Lord Ogilvy brought 300 men from Angus; the veteran John Gordon of Glenbucket as many from Aberdeenshire; Mackinnon of Mackinnon 120 from Skye. MacPherson of Cluny, who, like MacDonald of Lochgarry, had held a commission in Lord Loudon's regiment, was on the way with 300 of his followers, and Lord Lewis Gordon, a younger brother of the Duke of Gordon, was raising recruits from among his Grace's tenantry. The existing clan regiments were similarly strengthened by drafts of new men.

The Prince's small cavalry arm also received welcome additions. Lord Elcho, given command of a troop of Life Guards, 'Compleated it all of gentlemen of familly and fortune . . . their uniform blew and reed, and all extremely well mounted. . . .' Another newly-raised body of horse was commanded by the scholarly Lord Pitsligo. There were also Murray of Broughton's 'Hussars', wearing plaid waistcoats and fur caps, and a small troop commanded by Lord Kilmarnock, one of the few Lowland noblemen to join the Prince.

During October, hopes of foreign assistance were raised by the arrival of three French ships at Montrose and Stonehaven, bringing arms and other military equipment. This included 6 Swedish fieldguns of 2 to 4 pounds, which were added to Cope's captured train, and with them came 12 French gunners and Lieut.-Colonel James Grant, 'an able mathematician', whom the Prince appointed commander of the Jacobite artillery. Another arrival at this time was the Marquis d'Éguilles, an emissary of the French Court, to whom Charles accorded the title of French Ambassador.

Meanwhile, the Government had not been idle, for in addition to the 6,000 Dutch troops no fewer than 3 battalions of the Guards,

18 line regiments, 9 squadrons of cavalry, and 4 artillery companies had been ordered from Flanders. These, with the regular troops already in the country, had been formed into three army groups, which by the second half of October were moving into position. The first, commanded by Field-Marshal Wade, which included the Dutch, was on the march to Newcastle; the second, under Lieut.-General Sir John Ligonier, was destined for Lancashire; while the third, in expectation of a French landing, was taking up quarters along the south-east coast. Reinforcing these regular troops were the county militia, and a number of volunteer regiments raised for the emergency by enthusiastic Whig noblemen. One such unit was the Duke of Kingston's Light Horse, of which more will be heard.

Against these forces the Jacobite army could muster no more than 5,000 foot and 500 horse, and in considering its next move the Prince and his Council of officers were faced by two major 'unknowns'—French assistance and English support. To Charles the problem presented no difficulty. According to d'Éguilles, a French landing might be expected any day; as for the English, he was convinced that 'a great body . . . would join him upon his Entring their Country', and he proposed marching directly to Newcastle, and fighting Wade, 'for he was sure he would run away'. His Council, less sanguine, were against leaving Scotland, but the Prince remained adamant, and as a compromise Lord George Murray suggested marching into England through Cumberland, 'where, he Said, he knew the Country, That the Army would be well Situated to receive reinforcements from Scotland to join the French when they landed, or the English if they rose, and that it was a Good Country to fight Wade in, because of the Mountanious Ground . . .' It was, strategically, a sound plan, and having been approved by the Council, it was agreed to, after some demur, by the Prince.

Leaving Lord Strathallan at Perth in command of later reinforcements, the Highland army marched for England on the 3rd of November, in two divisions. The first, commanded by William Murray, the Jacobite Duke of Atholl, and the Duke of Perth, proceeded by Peebles and Moffat. The second, under the Prince and Lord George Murray, took a more easterly route by Lauder and Kelso, with the object of misleading Wade. The feint was completely successful, for thinking that the Prince intended to advance into England by way of Northumberland, the old Field-Marshal remained inactive at Newcastle. Instead, after a day's halt at Kelso, Charles swung westwards to Jedburgh, and marching down Liddesdale joined Atholl 4 miles north of Carlisle.

In the days of the Border wars Carlisle had been an important stronghold, but by 1745 its defences had become both obsolete and ruinous. A few weeks earlier Lieut.-Colonel Durand, a regular officer, had been ordered to see what could be done to strengthen them, and, among other improvements, 10 small 'ship guns' had been mounted on the town walls, as an addition to the Castle's 20 six-pounders. The regular garrison of the Castle consisted of 80 'invalids', most of whom were 'very old and infirm', a Master-Gunner and 4 gunners. Of the gunners, two were semi-trained civilians, and one a decrepit old man. Reinforcing these somewhat irregular 'regulars' were 500 foot and 70 horse of the Cumberland and Westmorland Militia, and some volunteer companies of towns-men. Another 120 townsmen had also been appointed as additional gunners.

The officers and men of the Militia were equally ill-disciplined, the former refusing to acknowledge Durand's authority on the ground that they were volunteers. The Mayor was a nonentity, and his deputy—one Alderman Thomas Pattinson—a conceited wind-bag. Only the clergy seem to have been dependable, and two kept watch from the Cathedral tower with 'a very large spying-glass' Durand had brought with him. To add to his troubles the Colonel was recovering from a severe attack of gout.

About noon on 9th November the vanguard of the Highland army, consisting of a party of horse, appeared to the north of the town, and shortly afterwards a countryman arrived with an order to the Mayor to provide quarters for 13,000 foot and 3,000 horse on the threat of reducing the place to ashes. To this no answer was returned, but the Castle guns opened fire on the party, and that night an express was sent to Wade, reporting the enemy's approach. Dawn next morning broke dark and foggy, but towards mid-day the weather cleared, and three Highland columns were seen approaching the town. They retired on the Castle guns again opening fire, and during the afternoon a summons was received 'from the Person stiling himself Prince Charles'. Written with the obvious intention of creating alarm and despondency, it called upon the inhabitants to open the gates 'to avoid the effusion of English blood', with the warning that otherwise 'it will not perhaps be in our Power to prevent the dreadful Consequences which usually attend a Town being taken by Assault'.

Leaving the citizens to ponder over their fate, the Highland army withdrew eastwards to Brampton on receiving a false report that Wade was on the march from Newcastle. By the 12th not a Highlander remained in sight of the town, and next day a letter arrived from Wade saying he was convinced that the rebels would not waste time in besieging Carlisle, but wishing the garrison 'all imaginable success'.

That same afternoon part of the Highland army returned to the town, and siege operations were immediately begun. These were directed by the Duke of Perth, while Lord George Murray, with six of the clan regiments, conducted a blockade, and next morning the inhabitants were alarmed to see a battery position being constructed 300 yards from the town walls. To calm their fears, Durand told them it was 'a poor paltry ditch, that did not deserve the name of an intrenchment', and ordered cannon to open fire on it.

The return of the Highlanders, coupled with Wade's letter was too much for the militia officers. It was clear, they said, that he was unable to come to the garrison's assistance, and they presented Durand with a round-robin declaring their intention of giving up the town. Their spirit of defeat soon spread to their men and the volunteers, and at a meeting of the townspeople it was agreed to join them in capitulating. After vainly protesting, Durand and the invalid officers retired into the Castle, having ordered the cannon on the town walls to be spiked. They were joined there by most of the militia officers, and a number of gentlemen, who were determined to defend it to the last, but during the night '. . . a mutiny begun among the private men of the Militia; who all declared they would do no more duty, nor would they stay and defend the Castle upon any account whatsoever. A general confusion ensued, numbers went over the walls; others forced their way out [of] the gates . . .', and by 8 o'clock next morning not one remained on duty.

Meanwhile, remembering Edinburgh, the Prince had threatened the citizens with fire and sword unless both town and Castle were given up, and unable to defend the Castle with the invalids alone, Durand gave way to the entreaties of the inhabitants and surrendered. The next day (16th November) Wade marched from Newcastle in a belated attempt to relieve the garrison. After two days' struggle through deep snow to reach Hexham he learnt that Carlisle had fallen, and returned to Newcastle with 1,000 sick men.

The siege had an unfortunate sequel, which might have had a disastrous effect on the Prince's fortunes. Ever since joining the Highland army at Perth, Lord George Murray had been only too well-aware that Charles both disliked and distrusted him, and he now resigned his commission as Lieutenant-General and announced his intention of serving as a volunteer. He is said to have resented the fact that he had not been kept informed of the negotiations leading up to the surrender, and that these had been entrusted to the Duke of Perth, a Roman Catholic, and to Murray of Broughton. While this may have been partly true, it is more probable that, realising the dangers confronting the Highland army, and that he alone was capable of leading it, Lord George demanded what amounted to a vote of confidence.

The news of his resignation was received by the principal officers with dismay. They petitioned the Prince that he 'Should be desired to take back his Commission', and Perth, to put an end to a dangerous situation, in turn resigned his Lieutenant-General's command during the Highland army's sojourn in England. As for some time there had been a 'dryness' between him and Lord George, Perth's action was all the more generous, but the fact that the Prince was thus forced to acknowledge Lord George's indispensability did nothing to improve Charles's relationship with his new commander.

With this crisis surmounted, the Prince's Council discussed future plans. Desertion had reduced the army by almost 1,000 men since leaving Edinburgh, and many of the members considered that it would be advisable to await reinforcements before proceeding further. The Prince, with his eyes fixed firmly on St. James's, had no doubts, and speaking 'with the more caution' on account of recent happenings, Lord George agreed with him. At the same time he made it clear that the extent of the advance must depend on what encouragement was received. Thus began one of the most remarkable adventures in British military history.

Having left a garrison of 100 men to defend the Castle, the Highland army marched from Carlisle in two divisions on 20th and 21st November.

'Lord George Murray commanded the first division, consisting of the low country regiments, such were generally called all except the clans, tho' the greatest part were Highlanders by their language, and all by their dress, for the Highland garb was the uniform of the whole army. Lord Elcho's guards marched always at the head of this division, and the foot regiments had the van by turns. The Prince commanded the second division in person, it consisted of the rest of the horse and the clans, who likewise had the van by turns. A part of the horse marched at the head of this division, and the rest brought up the rear of the whole army.'

Usually half a day's march separated the two divisions, for excepting in the larger towns there was insufficient accommodation for both; and although 'the Soldiers were lodged and gott their Victuals for nothing . . . the Officers payed for every thing they Gott, and very often extravagantly which they did rather than disoblige the people'.

Throughout the advance the Prince marched at the head of his division. 'He never dinn'd nor threw of his cloaths at night, eat much at Supper, used to throw himself upon a bed at Eleven o clock, & was up by four in the morning. As he had a prodigious strong constitution, he bore fatigue most surprisingly well.'

At each town King James's proclamation was read, but it aroused small enthusiasm, and the collection of the 'publick money' even less. Of Kendal, the best that could be said was that 'the people were civiler than in Cumberland'; at Lancaster, they 'testify'd no joy'; and it was not until reaching Preston—'vulgarly called Proud Preston, on Account of its being a Place of the best Fashion'—that there were heard 'for the first time in England several huzzas . . .'. Such qualified rapture produced no more than three gentlemen volunteers, of whom two were Welsh. The third, Francis Towneley, belonged to an old Lancashire family, and had seen service in the French army.

Manchester, of which the Prince expected great things, received him with bonfires, illuminations, and the sound of church bells—by order. A cheering crowd escorted him to his lodgings, and 'his Conversation that night at Table was, in what manner he should enter London, on horseback or a foot, and in what dress'. To his leading followers, however, his prospects of getting there were becoming more and more remote, and even O'Sullivan had begun to think of a retreat. 'We expected at least 1500 men wou'd have joyned us here', he wrote, but apart from a few gentlemen and merchants, the recruits amounted to no more than 'about 200 common fellows who it seems had no subsistance . . .'. They were, in fact, members of the local unemployed, who ingenuously explained that they had intended to join whichever army first reached Manchester. With the few other English recruits, they were formed into what was known as the 'Manchester Regiment', under the command of Francis Towneley.

In face of such discouragement there seemed little object in continuing the advance, but rather than risk the imputation of having failed to give the Prince their utmost support, Lord George and the chiefs agreed to 'make a further trial, and go the length of Derby . . .'.

So far, the Highland army had encountered no active opposition. The militia had vanished into thin air on its approach, and the only attempts to delay its progress had been by the breaking down of bridges. On the far side of the Pennines Marshal Wade and his army were slowly making their way southwards from Newcastle, and on the day after the Prince entered Manchester (30th November), had got no further than Catterick. Nearer at hand, the Duke of Cumberland, who had taken command of Ligonier's army, was concentrating his troops in the neighbourhood of Stafford, and threatened to bar the way to Derby.

The only means of avoiding a head-on collision with Cumberland was by giving him the slip, and leaving the Prince's division at Macclesfield, Lord George Murray turned off south-westwards to Congleton. Kingston's Light Horse, which had been posted there as an advance guard, hurriedly withdrew on his approach, and that night Murray sent forward a detachment under Colonel Ker of Graden towards Newcastle-under-Lyme, to collect information. This Ker did in the person of Captain Vere, the chief Government spy, who supplied Lord George with much valuable intelligence. It included a complete list of the Duke's army, which gave its numbers as 2,200 horse and 8,250 foot.

Thinking, as Lord George had hoped, that the Highland army intended to make westwards—possibly to Wales—Cumberland hastily withdrew his advanced troops and joined them with the rest of his army at Stone. The road to Derby was now clear, and turning again eastwards, Lord George marched by way of Leek to Ashbourne. On 4th December the Prince's division rejoined him at Derby.

15 James, titular 3rd Duke of Perth (From a contemporary portrait)

16 Lord John Drummond (From the portrait by Domenico Duprà)

17   The French Commanding Officer surrenders Carlisle to the Duke
of Cumberland (From an engraving by A. Miller after the painting by
Thomas Hudson, 1745)

18 The Earl of Albemarle (From the portrait by Thomas Hudson)

19 Lord Robert Kerr (From a portrait attributed to George Knapton)

20 Lord George Murray (From a contemporary portrait)

21 11th Regiment of Dragoons (From *A Representation of the Cloathing of His Majesty's Household*, 1742)

22 42nd Regiment of Foot (Highlanders)

23 34th Regiment of Foot

Both from *A Representation of the Cloathing of His Majesty's Household*, 1742)

24 'The Highland Chace, or the Pursuit of the Rebels': the Duke of Cumberland and his troops hasten to close with the Jacobite army

25 'John of Gant in Love, or Mars on his knees': a caricature published in 1749, during Cumberland's unpopularity after the suppression of the '45 (Both from contemporary prints)

26 Major-General William Blakeney (From an engraving by I. Faber after the painting by Thomas Hudson)

27 Dr. Archibald Cameron (From a contemporary engraving)

The question of whether or not to continue the advance could no longer be shelved, and next morning, while their men were crowding the cutlers' shops, 'quarrelling about who should be the first to sharpen and give a proper edge to their swords', the Jacobite leaders met at Exeter House, the Prince's headquarters. The debate was opened by Lord George. That night, he said, there could be little doubt that, having discovered his mistake, Cumberland would be at Stafford—as near London as Derby. Meanwhile, Wade was pushing on south by forced marches, and a third army was being formed for the defence of London. Together these three armies were over 30,000 strong, against the Prince's force of under 5,000 men, of whom none, including the Prince, would have the least chance of escape in the event of defeat. He concluded by saying that he considered the Scots had done their part. They had marched into England, to support either an English rising, or a French landing, but as neither had taken place, he advised a retreat to Scotland. An additional reason was the news that Lord John Drummond, the Duke of Perth's brother, had landed there with a French expeditionary force. Other members of the Council then expressed their views, and all were firmly of the same opinion.

The Prince sat listening to their arguments with ill-concealed impatience. According to Elcho, he 'fell into a passion and gave most of the Gentlemen that had Spoke very Abusive Language, and said that they had a mind to betray him'. In reply, however, he could offer few cogent reasons for continuing the advance. 'His Royal Highness', wrote Lord George Murray, 'had no regard for his own danger, but pressed with all the force of argument to go forward. He did not doubt but the justness of his cause would prevail, and he could not think of retreating after coming so far; and he was hopeful there might be a defection in the enemy's army, and that severals would declare for him.' Rather than retreat, Charles finally suggested marching into Wales, but not more than two of the Council supported this proposal, and the meeting broke up.

During the rest of the day the Prince made fruitless attempts to persuade the Council members to change their minds, and that evening a second meeting was held. Finding the Council's opinion unaltered, Charles bowed to the inevitable, but not with a good grace, exclaiming 'that for the future he would . . . neither ask nor take their Advice, that he was Accountable to nobody for his Actions but to his Father . . .'.

Early on 6th December the retreat was begun. To raise morale it was given out that the army was on its way to attack Wade, or, alternatively, to meet the French troops on the march from Scotland, but these stories carried little conviction, and the men were 'sullen and silent that whole day'. The rear-guard was commanded by Lord George Murray at his own request, his only stipulation being 'that the cannon and carriages with the ammunition, should march in the van . . . which was promised me'.

To simplify billeting arrangements the same route was followed as during the advance, but the Highland army's reception was now very different. At Manchester the advance-guard was threatened by an angry mob, and on leaving the town O'Sullivan was fired at in mistake for the Prince. Stragglers were set upon by the country-people, and either knocked on the head or dragged to the nearest gaol, and even the militia began to pluck up courage. In retaliation, the Highlanders, whose conduct during the advance had been exemplary, 'began to behave with less forbearance. And now few there were, who would go on foot, if they could ride; and mighty taking, stealing, and pressing of horses there was amongst us. . . .'

The Prince's chief anxiety was lest his enemies should look upon the retreat as a headlong flight, and it was only with difficulty that he was restrained from halting a day at Manchester. His own delaying tactics were a further source of worry to his rear-guard commander:

'We were commonly very late before the rear got to their quarters', comments Lord George. 'His Royal Highness, in marching forwards, had always been the first up in the morning, and had the men in motion before break of day, and commonly marched himself afoot; but in the retreat he was much longer of leaving his quarters, so that, though the rest of the army were all on their march, the rear could not move till he went, and then he rode straight on, and got to the quarters with the van.'

It was no time for such displays of pique, for although Cumberland's infantry had been marched almost to a standstill, he was pressing on in pursuit with all his available cavalry and 1,000 mounted foot. By 10th December he had reached Macclesfield, within two days' march of the Highland army, which was then at

Wigan, but a greater danger than 'Cumberland Will' was Wade, who on the same day was at Wakefield. It was thought certain that by marching into Lancashire, he would attempt to obstruct the Prince's line of retreat, and thus give Cumberland time to bring up the rest of his army. But Wade's infantry, like the Duke's, was in no condition to make rapid marches, and four cavalry regiments sent by him under Major-General Oglethorpe reached Wigan over icy roads, only to find that earlier that day the Highland army had marched towards Preston.

Before leaving Carlisle on the way south, orders had been sent to Lord Strathallan at Perth to bring up reinforcements, but these had met with no response. Determined not to abandon England without a struggle, the Prince sent off the Duke of Perth with still more urgent instructions, and at Lancaster insisted on halting for a day. At supper he 'talk'd much about retiring so fast', and next morning ordered Lord George and O'Sullivan to reconnoitre a field of battle. While doing so, their escort succeeded in capturing some of Oglethorpe's men, who confirmed the fact that only Wade's cavalry had been detached in pursuit, and that it had now linked up with Cumberland's at Preston.

It is likely that Charles's order to Lord George and O'Sullivan was no more than a piece of bravado, for on Murray reporting to him 'that, if our number would answer, I could not wish a better field for Highlanders: he said he was to march next day'. Perth's mission likewise came to nothing, for just short of Penrith he and his cavalry escort were attacked by militia, and forced to return to Kendal.

Knowing the state of the roads north of Preston, and the likelihood of their having been 'spoiled' still further by the country-people, Lord George had asked that two-wheeled ammunition carts might be substituted for the heavier four-wheeled waggons used on the better roads further south. Although this could have been done without difficulty, his request was ignored, and by the time Kendal was reached the cannon and ammunition waggons had fallen to the rear. On arriving there late at night he again applied to O'Sullivan for the change to be made, but the Adjutant-General was at supper with the Prince, and having 'got some mountain Malaga, which he seemed very fond of', was in no mood to be disturbed. The only satisfaction Lord George received was 'a glass or two of it', and next morning, 'a very bad, rainy day', all progress was stopped four miles north of Kendal by 'a water where there was a narrow turn and a steep ascent'.

Glengarry's men formed the rear-guard that day—'not the most patient, but I never was better pleased with men in my life', wrote Lord George—yet in spite of their efforts, and those of some officers of the Manchester regiment, who 'were up to the middle in water for an hour', there was nothing for it but to spend the night on the road. Fortunately there was a large farm nearby, and Murray and his men 'made the best shift we could, in the barns, byres, stables, and the farm house'.

At daybreak, having bought up all the small carts he could find, Lord George resumed his march. Somehow a rumour had reached the Prince 'of the amunition &c. being left behind', and during the morning two distinct orders were received from him 'not to leave, upon any account, the least thing, not so much as a cannon ball; for he would rather return himself, than there should be any thing left'. Swallowing his wrath, Lord George sent back a message, respectfully reminding the Prince of his broken promise, but assuring him he would 'do all that man could do'. Two miles farther on he carried out the Prince's instructions to the letter. For on finding one of the ammunition carts had fallen into a stream, he 'got the men to carry to Shap a good many cannon balls . . . I gave sixpence the piece for the doing it, by which means I got above two hundred carried'.

At Shap the rear-guard was joined by John Roy Stewart and his regiment, and next day, on the way to Penrith, there were signs of enemy activity. Small parties of horse were seen hovering in rear, and at one point 200 or 300 mounted militia drew up ahead, as if to engage, 'but so soon as the Glengary men threw their plaids, and ran forward to attack them, they made off at the top gallop . . .'. It seemed probable that these men were quartered in the vicinity of Lowther Hall, the seat of the Whig Lord Lonsdale, and on arriving at the village of Clifton Lord George sent forward the cannon and ammunition carts towards Penrith, while he with Glengarry's men scoured his Lordship's enclosures.

The militiamen were elusive, but 'at a turn of one of the parks, one like a militia officer, clothed in green, and a footman of the Duke of Cumberland's were taken'. The pursuit had at last caught up, for they reported that the Duke with 4,000 horse was only a mile behind. Having sent Roy Stewart in charge of the prisoners to Penrith, with a request for the Prince's instructions, Lord George and Glengarry's regiment returned to Clifton. There he found the Duke of Perth, who had arrived from Penrith with Cluny's and Ardshiel's regiments, and shortly afterwards a large body of enemy cavalry came into view south of the village, and drew up in two lines 'upon an open muir, not above cannon-shot from us'. Their smart appearance showed that the majority of them were no raw militiamen, and Perth offered to ride back to Penrith to bring up the rest of the army, but Lord George assured him that no more than 1,000 men were necessary.

The ground occupied by the Highlanders consisted of a series of hedged enclosures, intersected by a narrow lane leading to the village, and after Perth had gone on what proved to be a futile errand, Lord George 'caused roll up what colours we had, and made them pass half open to different places', in order to give the enemy an exaggerated idea of his numbers. It was now almost sunset, but Cumberland was in no hurry to attack, and it was not until an hour later that he ordered detachments from his three dragoon regiments —Bland's (3rd), Cobham's (10th), and Mark Kerr's (11th)—to dismount and advance on the Highlanders' position.

It was at this moment that Roy Stewart returned from the Prince. He reported that Charles intended to march immediately for Carlisle, and that his orders were that Lord George should retire to Penrith. 'As their was formerly a Contradiction to make the army halt when it was necessary to march', remarks Elcho sourly, 'so now their was one to march and shun fighting when their Could never be a better opportunity gott for it. . . .' To Lord George, the thought of retreating down the narrow lane in the darkness, followed by a further withdrawal along the road from Clifton, which was enclosed between high walls, had no attractions. There was bound to be confusion, and 'the enemy, by regular platoons in our rear . . . must destroy a great many; and by taking any wounded man prisoner, they would know our numbers; whereas . . . I was confident I could dislodge them from where they were by a brisk attack, as they had not, by all that I could judge, dismounted above five hundred'. Roy Stewart and Cluny agreed that this 'was the only prudent and sure way', and it was decided to say nothing about the Prince's order to the other officers.

It was now dark, but the moon shone fitfully from a cloudy sky, greatly to the advantage of the Highlanders, whose dark clothing made them less conspicuous than the dragoons. Posted in rear, nearest the village, was Roy Stewart's regiment, while the other three were drawn up behind some of the hedges separating the enclosures—Glengarry's to the right of the lane, the Stewarts of Appin and the MacPhersons to the left. Already, in Lord George's words, the enemy had been 'shooting popping shots', and part of them having crossed a ditch dividing the moor from the farthest enclosure, were making their way forward. The Highlanders advanced to meet them, and there was a sharp exchange of fire, although in the semi-darkness the two sides could do little more than aim at each other's musket-flashes.

On the right Glengarry's men met with little opposition, but on the left the MacPhersons, having given their fire, came under that of a party of dragoons lining the ditch. They were unprotected save for 'an open hedge', and led by Lord George Murray and Cluny with a shout of 'Claymore!', they drew their swords and charged forward on the enemy. Unlike their comrades at Prestonpans, the dragoons put up a stout resistance. The fact that they were wearing iron skull-caps may have given them additional confidence, for several Highlanders broke their swords over them. Before long, however, the dragoons were forced to give way, and fell back on their main body on the moor under the flank fire of Glengarry's regiment.

As usual the casualty figures are conflicting, but discounting a Whig report that the Jacobites attempted to conceal their dead by throwing 40 into the river Lowther, the killed on each side numbered about a dozen. The wounded were approximately double this figure, one of them being Lieut.-Colonel Honeywood of Bland's, who received three cuts on the head 'by neglect of putting on his scull capp'. By his own account Lord George Murray was lucky to have escaped inclusion in either list, for the bullets 'were so thick about me, that I felt them hot about my head, and I thought some of them went through my hair, which was about two inches long, my bonnet having fallen off'. There were also two or three bullet-marks on his targe, which had been lent him by old Glenbucket.

The skirmish was to have sinister repercussions, for in writing his report of it Cumberland mentioned that when some of the officers were wounded 'the Rebels cried, "No quarter! Murder them!" and they received several wounds after they were knocked down'.

On retiring to Penrith, Lord George found the Prince and the rest of the army on the point of marching off to Carlisle. Charles 'seemed very well pleased with what had happened', remarks Lord George, and he had every reason for being so. For the check to Cumberland put an end to the pursuit, and enabled the Highland army to reach Carlisle in safety.

Only a day was spent there, and before marching for Scotland it was decided to abandon all the artillery, with the exception of three of the Swedish field-guns. A far less defensible decision was that of leaving behind a Jacobite garrison of 400 officers and men under John Hamilton, the Duke of Gordon's factor, as Governor. Over a quarter of these unfortunates belonged to the Manchester regiment, the rest being drawn mainly from Perth's, Ogilvy's, Glenbucket's, and Roy Stewart's regiments. 'This was done against the opinion almost of Everybody but the Prince said he would have a town in England and he was sure the Duke could gett no Cannon to take it with.' Ten days later Cumberland battered the Castle into submission with the help of six 18-pounders brought from Whitehaven.

On 20th December—the Prince's 25th birthday—the Highland army marched to Longtown, where it crossed the swollen Esk. 'The foot marched in, six in a brest, in as good order, as if they were marching in a field, holding one another by the collars, every body & every thing past, without any losse but two woman, yt belonged only to the publick, yt were drownded.'

On reaching the farther bank the pipers played, and the men danced reels to dry themselves. They were on Scottish soil once more, and on Christmas Day the vanguard of the Highland army entered Glasgow.

5

Falkirk

WHILE THE Highland army had been in England, the military situation in Scotland had undergone considerable changes. A few days after it had crossed the Border, Cope's successor, Lieut.-General Roger Handasyde, had marched from Berwick with Price's (14th) and Ligonier's (59th) regiments, and the remains of Gardiner's and Hamilton's dragoons, and re-occupied Edinburgh. In the North, Lord Loudon, commanding part of his own regiment, and the 'independent companies' raised by Lord President Forbes, held Inverness for the Government; while in Argyll, the militia had been called out, and was being licked into shape by Major-General John Campbell of Mamore. Stirling Castle and the Highland forts still remained in Government hands, and at sea Rear-Admiral Byng's squadron kept a close watch on the east coast ports to prevent further arrivals of French troops and munitions.

At Perth, where Jacobite reinforcements had been assembling under Lord Strathallan, the Highland contingents included the Frasers, commanded by the Master of Lovat; the Earl of Cromarty with part of the Clan Mackenzie; the Farquharsons; and a regiment of Mackintoshes raised by Lady Mackintosh, whose husband, the clan chief, held a commission in the Black Watch. These had recently been joined by Lord John Drummond and the French troops, who had landed at Montrose, Stonehaven, and Peterhead. They consisted of his own regiment, the French Royal Scots, and detachments from the Irish Brigade, usually styled the 'Irish picquets'—in all some 750 men. With these additions Strathallan's force numbered between 3,000 and 4,000 men, thus being almost as large as the army that had marched to Derby.

At Glasgow, the capital of Scottish Whigdom, the Highlanders were met by sour looks, which became still sourer on the Prince demanding '6000 cloth short coats, 12000 linnen shirts, 6000 pair of shoes, 6000 bonnetts, and as many tartan hose, besides a sum of money'. After their long march his men were in desperate need of these articles, but apart from their necessity he had good reason for turning a deaf ear to the Magistrates' protests. For, while advancing on Edinburgh, he had demanded £15,000 from Glasgow, which was later reduced to £5,500, yet not content with having got off so lightly, the city had raised a militia regiment for Government service. Commanded by Lord Home, it was now stationed at Edinburgh with Price's, Ligonier's, and the two dragoon regiments.

Government fears of a large-scale French landing on the south coast were still very real, and having driven the Highland army out of England, the Duke of Cumberland was immediately recalled to take command of the anti-invasion forces. To follow up the pursuit and bring the Jacobites to action, a more dynamic commander than old 'Grandmother Wade' was clearly necessary, and on Cumberland's recommendation Lieut.-General Henry Hawley was appointed his successor.

In the course of his 50 years' service Hawley had earned an unenviable reputation for severity, and his nickname of 'Lord Chief Justice' was well merited. Quoting Horace Walpole, Lord Mahon describes how on one occasion in Flanders 'a deserter being hanged before Hawley's windows, the surgeons begged to have the body for dissection. But Hawley was reluctant to part with the pleasing spectacle; "At least", said he, "you shall give me the skeleton to hang up in the guard-room."' His military capacity was less apparent, for having fought at Sheriffmuir, where his regiment was posted on the victorious right wing, he had acquired the mistaken belief that Highlanders were unable to withstand a cavalry charge.

With the return of the Highland army from England there seemed every likelihood of Edinburgh receiving a second visit from the Prince, and during the last days of December the royal army began moving northwards from Newcastle. Marching in pairs, the first two regiments reached Edinburgh on 2nd January, the rest following at short intervals, until by the 10th a total of 12 battalions had been assembled. Excluding the two earlier arrivals, they consisted of the 2nd Battalion of the Royal Scots (1st), Howard's Old Buffs (3rd), Barrel's (4th), Wolfe's (8th), Pulteney's (13th), Blakeney's

(27th), Cholmondeley's (34th), Fleming's (36th), Munro's (37th), and Battereau's (62nd).

Meanwhile, the Jacobites had also been on the move. In addition to the French troops, Lord John Drummond had brought with him a train of artillery, which included two 16-pounders, two 12-pounders, and two 8-pounders. With these it was planned to reduce Stirling Castle, and marching eastwards from Glasgow on 3rd January, the Highland army took up quarters at Denny, St. Ninians, and Bannockburn. The town of Stirling was captured with little difficulty, for its walls had long since fallen into disrepair, and it was defended only by 500 militia and volunteers. Less simple was the problem of transporting the heavy guns from Perth, the largest of which weighed upwards of $1\frac{3}{4}$ tons, and required 20 'north country horses' to move them. Eventually, 'with great labour', two were brought to Stirling by way of the Fords of Frew, the rest being ferried over the Forth near Alloa, in spite of attempts by the Royal Navy and some of Hawley's troops to interrupt their passage.

The chief difficulty in attacking Stirling Castle was to find a battery position on anything approaching the level of the Castle guns, and according to Colonel Grant, the Prince's efficient artillery commander, there was only one suitable site. To this objections were made by the townspeople, and yielding to their protests, the Prince sought a second opinion. The person he consulted was a certain Mirabel de Gordon, a French officer of Scots descent, and a Chevalier of the Order of St. Louis, who had landed with Lord John Drummond. Although said to be 'one of the first Engineers in France', he is less flatteringly described by the Chevalier Johnstone:

> 'It was supposed that a French engineer of a certain age and decorated with an order must necessarily be a person of experience, talents, and capacity; but it was unfortunately discovered, when too late, that . . . he was totally destitute of judgment, discernment, and common sense. His figure being as whimsical as his mind, the Highlanders instead of M. Mirabelle, called him always Mr. Admirable.'

Another writer says he was 'always drunk'.

With blithe assurance M. Mirabel at once proceeded to open trenches for a battery position on the Gowan Hill, to the north of the Castle, where 'there was not fifteen inches depth of earth above the solid rock', and to remedy this defect large numbers of wool-packs and sand-bags had to be brought from a distance. Most of the constructional work was done by the French regulars, for the Highlanders considered it beneath their dignity, and the Lowlanders were more lazy than useful.

At Edinburgh, Hawley was also having his troubles. On arriving there on 6th January, he 'caus'd immediately two pair of Gallows to be set up; one in ye Grass Market, & the other between Leith and Edinr.' Having thus dealt with what he considered first matters first, he then proceeded to take stock of his army, and recorded his impressions in a series of letters to the Duke of Newcastle. Written in a large sprawling hand, they possess a certain uninhibited charm.

Of Hawley's 12 battalions, all but two—Ligonier's (59th) and Battereau's (62nd)—were 'old' regiments; moreover, of the 12, no fewer than nine, including Ligonier's, had been among those recalled from Flanders. In fact, however, his infantry was less formidable than appeared on paper. Some of the regiments, he complained, were 'no better than militia', and 'so weak that the twelve . . . make but 6600 men Rank and file fitt to marche . . .'. Moreover, after so much marching and countermarching under Wade, the foot were 'quite delabrée', and a week after his arrival Hawley wrote: 'I only beg of youre Grace not to call this yeat a considerable force in the Condition they are in. . . .'

Although one of the Prince's most cherished illusions was that he would be joined by large numbers of the royal troops, remarkably few actually did so, and only in the following case does there seem to have been any regular unit suspected of 'disaffection'. Two of Hawley's regiments, Battereau's and the 2nd Battalion of the Royal —known also by its Colonel's name as St. Clair's—had come from Ireland. On their embarking at Dublin the previous autumn, the Lord Lieutenant, Lord Chesterfield, had written to the Duke of Newcastle:

'I must acquaint your Grace, in Confidence, that when the Two Regiments embark'd here for England, there was a very great Difference observ'd in their Countenances, and Manner. That of Battereau's express'd great Willingness, and Alacrity, Whereas St. Clair's was sullen & gloomy. I could therefore wish, as I hinted to

Your Grace before, That It might have some other Destination, than that of going to Scotland.'

On the Royal landing in England, so the Bishop of Chester reported, 'a trusty Person' had been employed

'. . to feel the Pulse of the Common Men, and Such particularly as are Highlanders. Some of Them discovered great Unwillingness to go on that Business; Some said, They would not draw Their Sword, if They were sent there; They would not kill Their Father, or Their Brother, which, They said, might be the Case. How far this Spirit extends, I will not say. . . .'

Acting on these reports, it was at first decided to employ the regiment in the south of England, but as on further enquiry there appeared to have been 'little or no Foundation for Them', the Royal remained with Wade's army.

Besides 'the Glasgow Regt. of Enthusiasts', as Hawley described the militia, his army included two other volunteer units. One was an Edinburgh company, of which John Home was Lieutenant; the other, known as the 'Yorkshire Blues', had been raised at his own expense by William Thornton, a Yorkshire squire. It had as its fiddler 'Blind Jack' Metcalf of Knaresborough, who was afterwards to become famous as a roadmaker.

Hawley's cavalry consisted of Hamilton's and Ligonier's (late Gardiner's) dragoons. Neither numbered more than about 180 men, but he hoped shortly to be joined by Cobham's regiment, which had fought at Clifton. The two former, 'who are Cowed, whiche I don't reckon upon', remained as undisciplined as ever, and a few weeks earlier General Handasyde had reported that not only were they given to desertion, but had 'a damned Rebellious Spirit and a disposition to Rob Every where. . . . Of the two Hamilton's is much the worse.'

In spite of the object-lesson of Prestonpans, the state of the artillery was deplorable. The train was held up at Newcastle for want of horses, and at Edinburgh the only artillery personnel consisted of Fireworker Baillie Bryden, 'a boy of eighteen', and what remained of the party he had brought from Woolwich to man Cope's cannon. An application for the services of Major William Belford, who had commanded Cumberland's artillery at the recapture of

Carlisle, had been unsuccessful, for Belford had pled sickness—an excuse which Hawley considered far from genuine. 'The Major's sickness', he wrote, 'I suspect to be only a young Wife he wants to be withe. I know him. . . . He has sent me ane old Trooper of the Duke of Argille's, one Cuningham who is suche a Sott, and so ignorant that I beleive he and I shant agree long.' This prophecy was soon to be fulfilled.

Captain Archibald Cuningham had joined the Royal Regiment of Artillery in 1729 as a Cadet-Gunner. Sent for from Newcastle, where he had commanded the artillery company attached to Wade's army, he now found himself called upon to organise a 'scratch' train from whatever men and material were at hand. With the help of young Bryden he managed to scrape together '2 Bombardeers & 14 Unexperienc'd Mattrs: [Matrosses] and 12 Country People' with whom to man a miscellaneous assortment of cannon from Edinburgh Castle. These numbered 10, ranging from 1½- to 6-pounders, and the train also included a few small mortars.

All things considered, Hawley had at least some justification for his remark that '. . . nobody can worke without Tooles, and as to that point my situation is as bad as ever any bodyes was . . .'. It was therefore fortunate for him that he had an excellent second-in-command. Known to his men as 'Daddy', Major-General John Huske had a long and meritorious record of service, dating back to the wars of Queen Anne. More recently he had 'behaved gloriously' at the battle of Dettingen, where he had been severely wounded. He was a plain, honest man with few frills, who could be relied upon to use his initiative, and had 'a pleasure in instructing and taking care of young officers . . .'.

For all that on his own showing Hawley had the poorest opinion of the Highlanders—'I do and allwayes shall despise these Rascalls' —he had sufficient sense to realise that their method of fighting was something to which his troops were unaccustomed. He was also aware of the blood-curdling accounts of it which had been circulated, and with these considerations in mind, he issued the following directive in his orders dated 12th January:

'The manner of the Highlanders way of fighting which there is nothing so easy to resist If Officers & men are not preposess'd with the Lyes & Accounts which are told of them. They Commonly form their Front rank of what they call their best men, or True Highlanders,

the number of which being allways but few, when they form in
Battallions they commonly form four deep, & these Highlanders form
the front of the four, the rest being lowlanders & arrant scum.

When these Battallions come within a large Musket shot, or three
score yards, this front Rank gives their fire, & Immediately thro'
down their firelocks & Come down in a Cluster with their Swords
&Targets making a Noise & Endeavouring to pearce the Body, or
Battallions before them becoming 12 or 14 deep by the time they
come up to the people they attack.

The sure way to demolish them is at 3 deep to fire by ranks
diagonaly to the Centre where they come, the rear rank first, and even
that rank not to fire till they are within 10 or 12 paces but If the fire
is given at a distance you probably will be broke for you never get
time to load a second Cartridge, & if you give way you may give your
foot for dead, for they being without a firelock or any load, no man
with his arms, accoutrements &c. can escape them, and they give
no Quarters, but if you will but observe the above directions, they
are the most despicable Enimy that are.'

Although 'resolved to do nothinge rashely', Hawley was anxious
to come to grips with the enemy as soon as possible, and on 13th
January Huske marched westwards from Edinburgh with five
regular battalions, the Glasgow Militia, and Hamilton's and
Ligonier's dragoons. Of these, one regiment was detached to
Bo'ness, and the militia to Queensferry, while the rest under Huske
proceeded towards Linlithgow. Next day three more regiments were
sent to support him.

To cover the siege of Stirling Castle, part of the Highland army
under the Prince was now quartered in the neighbourhood of
Bannockburn, where he himself was staying at Bannockburn House
with Sir Hugh Paterson, an enthusiastic Jacobite. Also staying there
was Sir Hugh's niece, Clementina Walkinshaw, who was afterwards
to follow the Prince to France, and bear him a daughter. The rest of
the army, commanded by Lord George Murray, and consisting of
five clan regiments and part of the cavalry, was stationed nine miles
further eastwards at Falkirk.

Murray had been given timely warning of Huske's advance, and
when he heard that supplies for the royal troops were being collected
at Linlithgow, he determined to carry off or destroy as much of
these as he could. Early on the 13th he accordingly marched from

Falkirk with his division, and at Linlithgow sent forward the horse
under Elcho to patrol the roads leading to Edinburgh. About noon
Elcho reported that he had made contact with a small party of enemy
cavalry, which had fallen back on a larger body of horse and foot,
and two hours later Lord George was brought a further report 'that
their was a very large body of horse & foot advancing as fast as they
could . . .'. Having waited until the enemy had reached the outskirts
of the town, Lord George crossed the bridge over the Avon, half
a mile west of Linlithgow, planning to attack them 'when a half
should pass the bridge . . . but none of them passed it'. Instead, 'the
dragoons who was in the front of the regulars drew up close by the
Bridge and very abusive language pass'd betwixt both sides . . .'.
Not wishing to risk a fight with a general action impending, Lord
George withdrew to Falkirk, and next day received orders to rejoin
the Prince at Bannockburn. Kirkconnel writes:

> 'By this time most of the reinforcements were arrived from the
> North, or so near that they could not fail of being up before an action
> could happen. They looked mighty well, and were very hearty. The
> McDonalds, Camerons, and Stuarts, were almost double the number
> that had been in England. Lord Ogilvie had got a second battalion
> much stronger than the first. It was commanded by Sir James Kin-
> loch, Lt.-Colonel. The Frazers, Mackintoshes, and Farquharsons, were
> reckoned three hundred men each. The Irish piquets, and a part of
> Lord John Drummond's regiment, were already at Stirling; the rest
> of the regiment, and Lord Lewis Gordon's men, were within a day's
> march. The Earl of Cromarty, and his son Lord McLeod, were at
> Alloa, at the head of their own men. In fine, all were at hand in high
> spirits, and expressed the greatest ardour upon the prospect of a
> battle.'

Having decided that 'to go to Sterling without some Canon would
be silly', Hawley's movements were delayed by the train, which had
taken three days in getting from the Castle to Holyroodhouse. By
the 15th, however, it was ready to march, and with the rest of the
royal army proceeded westwards in the wake of the advance-guard.
Next day Hawley himself followed with Cobham's dragoons, and
by the evening of the 16th the royal army lay encamped in a field a
little to the west of Falkirk. It was joined there next morning by
Lieut.-Colonel John Campbell, who had marched from Glasgow
with three companies of Lord Loudon's regiment, one of Lord John

Murray's (Black Watch), and 12 of the Argyll Militia. Including Campbell's troops the royal army numbered approximately 8,500 men.

Unlike the Highlanders, who were quartered over a wide area in small detachments, the royal troops could be rapidly concentrated, and there was the obvious danger that should Hawley suddenly advance, he might succeed in defeating the Prince's army in detail. The shorter the distance between the two armies, the greater this risk became, and on the morning of 15th January the Highlanders drew up in order of battle on Plean Muir, two miles south-east of Bannockburn, to await reports of the enemy's movements. The same procedure was followed next day, but apart from the arrival of Hawley's main body, the Jacobite patrols had nothing to report, and early that afternoon the Highlanders returned to their quarters.

On the 17th the Highland army drew up for the third time on Plean Muir. In spite of orders issued the previous night, it was almost mid-day before all the men were assembled, and with the royal army so close at hand it was clear that this state of affairs could not be allowed to continue. Having reviewed his troops, the Prince accordingly called a council of war, at which Lord George Murray proposed that, instead of waiting to be attacked, the Highland army should take the offensive. Reports already received that morning indicated that the enemy had no immediate intention of moving, and knowing the Highlanders' preference for high ground, he suggested as their objective 'the hill of Falkirk', a ridge of bare moorland rising steeply to the south-west of the town. The ridge lay about a mile from Hawley's camp, and Lord George, who knew the ground well, was convinced that, as the Highland army's advance would be unexpected, it would have no difficulty in gaining the top of the hill before the royal troops.

This proposal having been approved by the Prince and the rest of the officers, plans were made for it to be immediately carried out, for there was no certainty of how long the enemy might remain quiescent. To distract attention from the movements of the Highland main body, it was decided that Lord John Drummond, with part of his own regiment, the Irish picquets, and all the cavalry should take the main road leading from Bannockburn to Falkirk. This passed to the north of the Torwood, the remains of the old Caledonian forest, at which point his force could be clearly seen from the enemy's camp. Meanwhile, marching by side roads and across fields, and by making a considerable detour, it was hoped that the main body would be able to advance unnoticed until it reached the ford over the river Carron, little more than two miles from Falkirk. As a final touch, it was arranged that the Prince's standard should be left flying on Plean Muir.

These details settled, the advance was begun between 12 and 1 o'clock. Marching in two parallel columns, 200 yards apart, the left-hand column, under Lord George Murray, was headed by the three Clan Donald regiments, whose turn it was to occupy the right of the line. Led by the Atholl Brigade, the right-hand column was commanded by the Prince. As between 1,000 and 1,200 men had been left under the Duke of Perth to cover the siege of Stirling Castle, the Highland army's strength was slightly less than Hawley's, namely about 8,000 men.*

On his arrival at Falkirk the previous night Hawley had established himself at Callendar House, the seat of the Jacobite Lord Kilmarnock, about three-quarters of a mile to the east of the town. To Lady Kilmarnock he must have been a far from welcome guest, but disguising her feelings, she played the part of genial hostess with such success that she was to contribute not a little to his defeat. To make room for him and his staff, some of the Glasgow Militia officers were turned out of their beds, and one, William Corse, describes the General's movements the following morning. According to his account, Hawley rode over to the camp about 5 o'clock, and at 10 'went out to a little eminence on the left of the Camp, & 500 yards nearer the Enemy, to reconnoitre the Grounds between our Camp & ye Torwood; where I heard some of the Officers say, they saw them moving on this side the Torwood Southwards. This proved true; though I saw nothing, neither did Mr. Hawley.' Having apparently satisfied himself that there was no major movement on the part of the enemy, Hawley returned to Callendar House. The last thing he expected was that the Highland army would dare to attack him, and in this false sense of security he considered it unnecessary to send out regular cavalry patrols to collect information.

About 11 o'clock a body of the enemy's horse and foot was seen

* Government intelligence reports estimated the Highland army's strength as between 6,000 and 6,500 men. See also Hawley's letter to Cumberland, *post*.

moving about to the north of the Torwood with their colours and standards, and the royal army stood to arms. This body, acting as a covering force, was soon ordered to return to Plean, and having been stood-down after a quarter of an hour, Hawley's men went in search of dinner. This, according to Corse, 'was not easy to be found', and must have taken still longer to prepare, for they had barely finished their meal, when, shortly before 1 o'clock, an excited countryman rushed into the camp, shouting, 'Gentlemen, what are you about? The Highlanders will be immediately upon you!' Climbing a tree, two officers of the 3rd (Old Buffs) soon verified his report by means of a telescope, through which the main body of the Highland army could clearly be seen approaching to the south of the Torwood. Their commanding officer, Lieut.-Colonel Howard, at once rode off with this information to Callendar House, but Hawley seemed quite unable to grasp its significance. So convinced was he that the royal army was in no danger of attack, that he considered it unnecessary to return to the camp, and merely gave orders that the men were to put on their equipment, but that there was no need for them to stand to arms.

Had Hawley but known it, the Highland army's march had been in some danger of being abandoned. For having covered about half a mile:

'Mr. O'Sullivan came up to me [wrote Lord George] and told me he had been talking with the Prince, and that it was not thought advisable to pass the water in sight of the enemy, and therefore it was best delaying it till night, and then we could do it unperceived. This surprised me; I told him that we could be all past the water in less than a quarter of an hour, and the place we were to pass, was two full miles from the enemy. I did not halt, and he went back to his Royal Highness, who was riding betwixt the two lines.'

A little later the Prince rode up with Brigadier Stapleton, the commander of the Irish picquets, O'Sullivan, and some of the other officers. Still keeping on the march, Lord George pointed out the impossibility of the men lying out all night at that time of year, and that if such a plan were attempted, they would merely disperse and look for shelter. Either they should continue the advance, or return to their quarters, 'for it seemed to threaten a very bad night'. On Stapleton agreeing that unless the enemy was sufficiently near to dispute the crossing there could be no danger, Lord George replied that 'so far from disputing our passing . . . we were now within half a mile of the water, which then was very small, and that the enemy were two full miles off, and could not see us till we were very near it . . .'. This settled the argument, although Lord George was happily unaware that the Highland army had already been observed, and that it was solely due to Hawley's negligence that no steps had been taken to interrupt its advance.

Between 1 and 2 o'clock a party of volunteers rode into the royal camp 'upon the spur'. They brought news that the Highlanders were about to ford the Carron at Dunipace Steps, with the evident intention of making for the high ground on Falkirk Muir, and ordering the drums to beat to arms, Huske hurriedly sent off a messenger to Callendar House. Corse wrote:

'I never was used to these things; but I was surpriz'd to see in how little time ye regular troops were form'd (I think in less than half an hour) on ye left of ye Camp, in two Lines, with the Dragoons on ye flanks; all fronting the South, & just along the side of the high road leading to Stirling, the Road in their front, & Falkirk on their left.'

Meanwhile, 'one might hear the officers saying to one another, where is the General? what shall be done? we have no orders', and among them was Captain Cuningham. Earlier that morning he had gone to Falkirk 'to Shave & Shift himself, for he had no Tent in ye Camp, haveing been obliged to leve that at Newcastle', and when the army formed he took post on the left with the train. Having no orders, he went in search of Hawley, but being unable to find him, he rode over to Huske on the right for instructions. All Huske could do, however, was to refer him to Hawley, and Cuningham returned to the left where he stood waiting in front of the guns.

Long afterwards an old woman remembered how, as a child, she and the rest of her family had been taken for safety to Falkirk from an outlying farm. While passing through the royal army lines, a hare had started up, 'upon which the soldiers raised a loud *view-hollo*, and one, more ready-witted than the rest, exclaimed "Halloo, the Duke of Perth's mother!"—it being a general belief that that zealous old Catholic lady was a witch and therefore able to assume the disguise of a hare . . .'. The Highlanders were not alone in having 'freits'.

The sudden arrival of Hawley at the gallop, without his hat, and with what Chambers describes as 'the appearance of one who has abruptly left a hospitable table', can have done little to inspire his troops with confidence. Realising at long last the seriousness of the situation, he now made desperate efforts to retrieve it, and hastily ordered forward the cavalry, followed by the foot and artillery, in the hope of being able to forestall the Highlanders in reaching the summit of the moor.

The field of battle, which Hawley was about to see for the first time, presented a striking contrast to that of Prestonpans. From its lower slopes on the outskirts of the town, the hill rose steeply to a moorland plateau of scrub and heather, on which were a few scattered farms surrounded by small patches of cultivated land. The face of the hill was made up of irregular folds and ridges, intersected by a deep ravine, running half-way up the hillside. This gully was to play an important part in determining the course of the battle.

Led by Ligonier's (late Gardiner's) the three dragoon regiments crossed the Stirling road, and skirting the east wall of the Bantaskin House enclosures by a lane, known as 'Maggie Wood's Loan', began climbing the steep ascent. They were under the command of Colonel Francis Ligonier, who in addition to being Colonel of the 59th Foot had recently succeeded the dead Gardiner as commanding officer of the 13th Dragoons. A younger brother of Lieut.-General Sir John Ligonier, he possessed the same sense of duty, for he was suffering from pleurisy, and had taken the field against his doctor's orders.

Following the cavalry in column of route came Hawley's front-line troops, consisting of Wolfe's, Cholmondeley's, Pulteney's, The Royal, Price's, and Ligonier's regiments. His second line, forming the rear column, was composed of Blakeney's, Munro's, Fleming's, Barrel's, Battereau's, and Howard's (Old Buffs).

As Lord George Murray had predicted, a storm was not far off. The sky had become overcast, and a strong wind was blowing from the south-west. To make certain that it would be behind the Highland army on its forming line, he had made a wide circuit after crossing the Carron, and marching 'very quick' the two parallel columns breasted the hillside. Hidden from them by the configuration of the ground, the dragoons were hurrying up it from the opposite direction, and it was not until the two sides had almost reached the summit that they came in sight of each other. To the Highlanders it at first appeared that the enemy were merely a reconnoitring party, but soon more and more horse came into view.

'The Dragoons made several motions towards the front of Ld Georges Colum, and by coming very near often Endeavour'd to draw of the highlanders fire but to no purpose, for they marched on until they came to a bog, and then the whole army wheel'd to the left. . . .'

There now followed a pause of 'a full quarter of an hour', and during this interval the three MacDonald regiments advanced very slowly in line, 'foot by foot', to allow the other regiments time to come up on their left. Lord George had chosen to fight on foot, and with broadsword and targe he walked down the line, desiring the men 'to keep their ranks, and not to fire till he gave the order. All this was executed with as much exactness as was possible, and as sometimes one part of the line was farther advanced than the rest, they halted till the others came equal to them.' As a further precaution he sent his two mounted A.D.C.s, Colonel Ker and young Anderson of Whitburgh, to reconnoitre the dragoons, and on their return they reported that they were unsupported by infantry.

Meanwhile, having formed line as they came up, the Jacobite centre and left-wing regiments extended down the hillside from the comparatively level ground near the summit occupied by the right. On the extreme left were the Stewarts of Appin, who had taken up position near the mouth of the ravine, and between them and the three MacDonald regiments on the right were posted the Camerons, Frasers, MacPhersons, Mackintoshes, Mackenzies, and Farquharsons. The second-line regiments, in the same order, were those of Lord Lewis Gordon and Lord Ogilvy, each of two battalions, and the three battalions of the Atholl Brigade. The troops detailed as a reserve arrived later. They were those which had accompanied Lord John Drummond on his feint march, and on coming up they formed in rear of the second line, under the command of the Prince. The French regulars were posted in the centre, with the cavalry on either side, being 'not well mounted enough to resist the choc of the enemys horse'.

'As the front line was much more than double of either the other two', notes Kirkconnel, 'there were very large intervals betwixt the centre and wings of the second and third line.'

In arranging the Jacobite order of battle that morning there had been a remarkable omission, which was to have serious consequences. For in spite of Lord George Murray's having twice asked

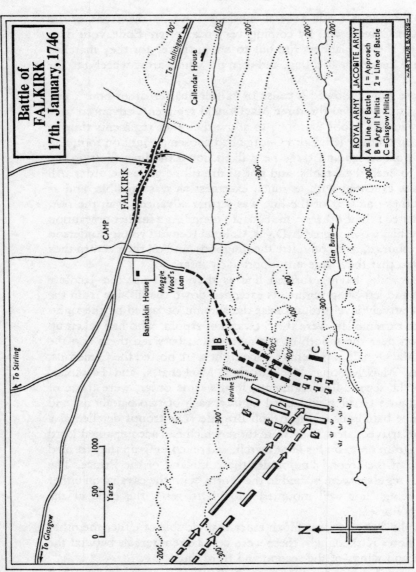

Battle of
FALKIRK
17th. January, 1746

ROYAL ARMY
A = Line of Battle
B = Argyll Militia
C = Glasgow Militia

JACOBITE ARMY
I = Approach
2 = Line of Battle

—ARTHUR BANKS

Referring to the 'official' plans of the battle, two of which were drawn by John Elphinstone and William
Cuninghame, the Scots Magazine comments: 'The line of dragoons was pretty near due South and North; the
front-line of the foot was likewise straight, it formed an angle at the South-end with the line of dragoons, and

'that his Royal Highness would appoint the officers that were to command, and where', this had not been done. Even he himself had been given 'no particular charge' beyond that of leading the front-line troops, from which he had inferred that he was expected to command the right wing. As a result, the post of left-wing commander remained unfilled, for although nearly all accounts of the battle describe Lord John Drummond as occupying that position, 'yet I believe', wrote Lord George, 'he had no directions to do it, and was not there when the battle began'.

While the Highland army was forming, O'Sullivan was sent by the Prince 'to arrange' the front line. On his arrival at the right he as usual proceeded to criticise Lord George Murray's dispositions; the ground nearby was 'full of old stone walls, & . . . one of them just at the heels of his last rank'. He consequently advised him to move forward to another wall, 'wch was the greatest advantage he cou'd have', and to this Murray agreed. To a further suggestion that, as his flank was uncovered, he should order the Atholl Brigade to advance in column to cover it, 'Ld George wou'd not hear to yt'. As, according to his own account, the right wing was protected by 'a small morass', Lord George's decision was hardly surprising.

During their ascent of the hill the dragoons had gained a considerable lead over the royal infantry, which was still pressing on behind them as the Highland army formed line of battle. Still further behind was Captain Cuningham, who had been ordered to march the train in rear of the leading column, but who was unable to keep up with it. When the second column overtook him soon afterwards, 'two of his biggest Guns in ye front stuck in a Bog, wch he could not disengage by any Endeavours he could at that time use, neither could he bring forwards any of the Guns that were behind except 2 : 4 pounders & one 1½ pounder'. He was still struggling to bring them up when the action began. The Prince's artillery was in no better plight. Trailing along far in rear of the Highland army, it never reached the field.

Since it proved impossible to outflank the Jacobite right on account of the marshy ground, the dragoons made further attempts 'to draw the fire, and ride in and break the Highlanders', but these were no more successful than before. Remembering Lord George's instructions, the MacDonalds refused to be tempted, and the three regiments finally took position facing the Highland front line. So wide were the intervals between their squadrons that, although Ligonier's was drawn up opposite Keppoch's regiment on the Jacobite right, the right-hand squadron of Hamilton's almost fronted the Jacobite centre.

The storm, which had long been threatening, now broke, and as the royal foot toiled up the hillside, the rear regiments 'running & quite out of breath wh the fatigue', the rain came down in torrents. Driven by the high wind, it lashed the faces of the troops, drenching their cartridges, so that when the engagement began one in four of their muskets missed fire. Hastily forming line, Wolfe's, the leading regiment, took up position to the right of Hamilton's, and the rest stationed themselves on Wolfe's right as they came up. Following the front-line troops, Hawley's second-line regiments, led by Blakeney's, drew up in rear, although eye-witnesses mention that some of the late-comers had not completed this movement when the action began. As Howard's, the rear-most regiment, was ordered to fall back in reserve, the second line eventually consisted only of five regiments.

The Glasgow regiment being considered insufficiently trained to be given a place in the line, 'march'd up the Hill very stoutly', and took post near some cottages, well in rear of the dragoons. It was to see more of the battle than the Argyll Militia, who 'were posted, or posted themselves' on the far right, near the bottom of the hill.

In their final position, the opposing lines of foot presented an odd contrast. For, whereas on the left the royal infantry was outflanked by half the Jacobite front-line regiments, the situation on the right was the reverse, although to a lesser extent. Moreover, the fact that the three right-wing regiments—Price's and Ligonier's in the front line, and Battereau's in rear—were drawn up facing the ravine prevented them from working round the Jacobite left. To the Camerons and Stewarts, however, their presence was far from reassuring, and when O'Sullivan came over to the left with orders, 'one Daniel Cameron answer'd yt all he said shou'd be executed, if he'd answer, yt they shou'd not be outwinged'. O'Sullivan 'did not like yt reflection'. Farther to the left he was alarmed to find that the enemy was forming what he calls 'a hollow square of at least four Battaillons'. Keeping 'the dread he was in' to himself, he at once sent an A.D.C. to bring up Lord Ogilvy's regiment from the second line, but probably because the order was given too late, it was not carried out. Lord George Murray, who was evidently unaware of this order of O'Sullivan's, later blamed him for having taken no action in his capacity as Adjutant-General. But, as he himself emphasises more than once, the real need was a senior officer in command of the left wing, for 'had there been men brought up, either from the second line on the left, or the corps de reserve, to have faced these regiments that outlined the Highlanders, the battle would not have lasted ten minutes . . .'.

It was now nearly 4 o'clock, and the light was already beginning to fade, when without waiting until all his infantry was formed, Hawley sent orders to Colonel Ligonier to begin the attack. His faith in the superiority of cavalry over Highlanders was evidently not shared by the Colonel, who showed the greatest astonishment at his instructions. Advancing on the Highland right, the three regiments came down 'at the full trot, in very good order'. Lord George Murray waited until they were within pistol shot before he raised his musket as the signal to fire. Delivered at a range of 10 yards the Highlanders' volley was devastating. About 80 dragoons fell dead on the spot, and Corse, who watched the attack from the Glasgow regiment's position in rear, says that 'in one part of them nearest us I saw day light through them in several places'.

On receiving the Highlanders' fire, most of the troopers turned and fled. An honourable exception was a small party of Ligonier's men, led by Lieut.-Colonel Whitney, the officer formerly wounded at Prestonpans. As they advanced to the attack he recognised Colonel John Roy Stewart and shouted to him, 'Ha! are you there? We shall soon be up with you.' 'You shall be welcome when you come', replied Stewart, 'and, by God, you shall have a warm reception.' A few moments later Whitney fell dead, but inspired by his example his men broke into the ranks of Clanranald's regiment.

> 'The most singular and extraordinary combat [writes Johnstone] immediately followed. The Highlanders, stretched on the ground, thrust their dirks into the bellies of the horses. Some seized the riders by their clothes, dragged them down, and stabbed them with their dirks; several again used their pistols; but few of them had sufficient space to handle their swords. Macdonald of Clanranald . . . assured me that whilst he was lying upon the ground, under a dead horse, which had fallen upon him, without the power of extricating himself, he saw a dismounted horseman struggling with a Highlander:

fortunately for him, the Highlander, being the strongest, threw his antagonist, and having killed him with his dirk, he came to his assistance, and drew him with difficulty from under his horse.'

On the repulse of the cavalry, Lord George Murray ordered the three MacDonald regiments to stand their ground, but it was impossible to restrain Glengarry's and Clanranald's men, and, sword in hand, they rushed off in pursuit of the runaway dragoons. Galloping to the rear, 60 of Hamilton's troopers blundered into the Glasgow regiment, '& carry'd off about a Company of our people; among whom I was', wrote Corse, '& would then have given my life for a shilling. Some of us they rode over, and some of us ran and rode so well that we got quit of them in about 5 or 600 yards, with the utmost difficulty.' In the same blind panic Ligonier's and the rest of Hamilton's regiment broke away down the hillside, plunging into the royal left wing, and scattering men in all directions, while Cobham's, riding off between the two armies, came under fire from the Jacobite centre and left.

'It was', as Kirkconnel wrote, 'a fine beginning; but the first success had like to have cost very dear', for carried away by the excitement of the chase the two MacDonald regiments were incapable of being rallied. 'Some pursued the dragoons, others fell a plundering the dead; a considerable body that kept a just direction in their march, fell in with the Glasgow militia, and were employed in dispersing them.' From the Jacobites' point of view, it was a miserable waste of two of their best regiments.

On the left, the rout of the dragoons had created a still more serious situation, for the men of the front-line regiments had expended most of their fire on Cobham's, and now found themselves unable to reply to that of the royal foot. The heavy rain, and the fact that the Highlanders did not use cartridges, made re-loading impossible, and with what O'Sullivan calls 'perhaps one of the boldest and finest actions, yt any troops of the world cou'd be capable of', they flung down their muskets, and charged forward sword in hand. Breaking their ranks, many of the men in the second-line regiments followed hard on their heels. Attacked in front and in flank, Hawley's left-wing troops, already disordered by the dragoons, and half-blinded by the rain, offered little resistance. After giving a weak and ineffectual fire, four of his six front line-regiments—Wolfe's, Cholmondeley's, Pulteney's, and the Royal—turned and ran, and they were almost immediately followed by the whole of the second line, with the exception of Barrel's. So sudden and unexpected was their disappearance that when he saw the flight of the Royal, Lord John Drummond exclaimed: 'These men behaved admirably at Fontenoy. Surely this is a feint.'*

John Home, who with the Edinburgh volunteer company was drawn up some distance in rear of Fleming's regiment, watched the rout of the royal infantry. Seeing Hawley, 'involved in a crowd of horse and foot', he somewhat tactlessly chose this moment to ask him 'if there were any regiments standing? Where they were? The General made no answer'—probably for obvious reasons—'but pointing to a fold for cattle which was close by, called to him to get in there with his men. The disorder and confusion encreased, and General Hawley rode down the hill.'

Luckily for Hawley, three of his regiments were made of sterner stuff, and although he himself had lost all control of the situation, Huske kept his head. Protected by the ravine in front of them, Ligonier's men, commanded by Lieut.-Colonel Stanhope, 'a fine lively young lad', stood their ground, as did Price's on their left. Barrel's, likewise, remained firm, and when it had joined the two front-line regiments, all three moved up the hill towards the left. Taking up position under the orders of Huske and Brigadier Cholmondeley, they poured in a heavy fire on the flank of the pursuing clansmen, which 'threw them into great disorder'. To add to the confusion, Colonel Roy Stewart, 'afraid lest this might be an ambuscade . . . called out to the Highlanders to stop their pursuit; and the cry of stop flew immediately from rank to rank . . .'. Shaken and uncertain what to do next, some of the men stood still, while others returned to the ground on which they had formed. Many, even, left the field, and hurried back to Bannockburn and Stirling where they gave out that the Highland army had been defeated.

Out of sight on the ridge above, Lord George Murray, and what remained with him of Keppoch's regiment, had been joined by the Atholl Brigade. Alone of the second line, its three battalions had kept their ranks, and advancing down the hill with them 'in perfect good order', he determined to attack the fleeing enemy, who could be seen 'running off by forties and fifties to the right and left to get

* It was, in fact, the 1st Battalion which fought at Fontenoy.

into Falkirk . . .'. Collecting stragglers as he went, Lord George sent
off Colonel Ker 'to entreat that the reserve might advance on the
left', and such support became all the more necessary on the
reappearance, soon afterwards, of Cobham's regiment. Having
rallied, the dragoons marched up the hill with the apparent intention
of getting to the rear of the Jacobite position. It was thought that
they were hoping to capture the Prince, but if so, they were to be
disappointed. For either on Charles's own initiative, or in response
to Ker's request, the Irish picquets were moved forward from the
reserve, and at the sight of their advance, Cobham's fell back on the
three right-wing regiments. Forming a rear-guard, the dragoons
retired with them in good order towards Falkirk.

On their way, they came upon the royal train, lying abandoned at
the bottom of the hill, for the civilian drivers of all but three of the
gun teams had fled with their horses when the left-wing regiments
were routed. With the exception of a solitary matross, they were
immediately followed by the rest of Cuningham's men, and having
returned down the hill with the three smaller guns, he had then
retired to Falkirk. Barrel's showed more initiative; the grenadiers
harnessed themselves to one of the guns and succeeded in dragging
it away. Two more were subsequently recovered by horse-teams
from Falkirk. When later he thanked the regiment for its good conduct, wrote a private, 'Brigadier —— was pleased to express his
Satisfaction in our Behaviour, by kissing our Men, and making us
a Present of ten Guineas.'

With 'not above six or seven hundred men with him, the rest
being all scattered on the face of the hill', Lord George thought it
inadvisable to follow up the royal rear-guard and having been joined
by Lord John Drummond with the reserve, he halted at the bottom
of the hill. It was now almost dark, and the most urgent question
was where the Highland army should be quartered for the night.

'Most were of the opinion to retreat towards Dunnipace and the
places adjacent, where the men might be covered, it being a prodigious
rain; but Lord George Murray was absolutely for marching into the
town, for he said that if the enemy had the least time, they might line
the houses, and clean their guns, so as to make it impossible . . .
and that, therefore, there was not one moment to be lost, for he was
certain the enemy were in the utmost confusion; and concluded with
Count Mercy's expression at the battle of Parma, that he would either

lye in the town or in paradise. His Royal Highness came up at that very time, and approved much of the resolution of attempting the town, and was advised himself to stay at some house in the face of the hill, till Lord George Murray sent him word of the success.'

Fortunately for Lord George, the choice of Falkirk or Paradise did not arise, although for some time the enemy's intentions remained uncertain. Fires seen burning in their camp suggested that the royal army intended to spend the night there, but a report from Lord Kilmarnock ended all uncertainty. Making good use of his local knowledge, he had ridden towards the high road leading to Linlithgow, along which he had seen the royal army hurrying off in full retreat. The subsequent 'official' explanation of this withdrawal was more plausible than convincing:

> 'The evening being excessive rainy, it was thought proper to march the troops to Linlithgow that night, and put them under cover; otherwise we should have continued in our camp, being masters of the field of battle, and Brig. Mordaunt was ordered to take post there. When we came to strike our tents, we found that many of the drivers had run off with the horses: upon which the General gave orders, that what tents were left should be burnt; which was done.'

Joined by Lochiel, Keppoch, and some of the other senior officers, Lord George with the Athollmen, and Lord John Drummond with the French troops, entered Falkirk from opposite ends of the town. It was found that 'most of the enemy were gone, there being but few taken prisoners there'. Lord John was wounded in an attempt to capture a straggler. On seizing the man, 'the souldier strugled wth him, got off, fired at him, & shot him in the Arm'. The Prince entered Falkirk soon afterwards, and 'profited of General Hally's supper wch he wanted very much'. O'Sullivan also mentions with obvious relish that 'a great many hampers of good wines, & liquors & other provisions were found in the Town'.

At the camp it was discovered that the clumsy attempts of Hawley's troops to set fire to their tents had been far from successful, and that most of them were still standing. All the ammunition and a large number of waggons were also taken, and the captures included 'three standards, two stand of colours, a kettledrum, many small arms, their baggage, clothing, and generally every thing they had not burnt or destroyed'.

There could be no question of pursuing the enemy, for apart from the darkness and the pouring rain, the Highland army was by now widely dispersed. According to Lord George, 'fifteen hundred men in all came in that night', and barely enough could be found to provide guards for the town. Many of the Highlanders were engaged in pillaging the dead, and ransacking the camp, while still larger numbers had returned to their old quarters near Bannockburn, knowing nothing of the outcome of the battle. Even some of the regimental commanders were uncertain of the result until informed of it by MacDonald of Lochgarry about 8 o'clock that night.

Like Prestonpans, the action at Falkirk lasted a very short time, and Home says that, on comparing notes, some of the Jacobite officers and their prisoners agreed that not more than 20 minutes elapsed between the firing of the first shot and what he calls the retreat of Barrel's regiment. Jacobite casualties were small. The killed amounted to about 50, of whom seven were junior officers, and the wounded to between 60 and 80. In addition to Lord John Drummond, the latter included Lochiel and his brother, Archibald Cameron, both of whose wounds were slight.

Hawley's losses were far greater than his official return of 12 officers and 55 men killed, and his grand total of 280 'killed, wounded, and missing'. Home's comparable figures under 'killed' are 16 officers and 300 to 400 men, and Elcho's—the highest Jacobite estimate—30 officers and 500 to 600 men. The casualties among the senior officers were unusually heavy, and the dead included Sir Robert Munro, the commanding officer of the 37th, and his second-in-command, Lieut.-Colonel Biggar; Lieut.-Colonel Powell of Cholmondeley's; and the gallant Whitney of Ligonier's Dragoons. Nor did Colonel Ligonier long survive the battle, for having been soaked to the skin, he contracted a quinsy of which he died a few days later.

As head of his clan and a stout-hearted soldier, Sir Robert's death was regretted by both sides. His son wrote:

> 'My father, after being deserted, was attacked by six of Locheal's Regt, and for some time defended himself wt his half Pike. Two of the six, I'm inform'd he kill'd; a seventh, coming up, fired a Pistol into my father's Groin; upon wch falling, the Highlander wh his sword gave him two strokes in the face, one over the Eyes & another on the mouth, wch instantly ended a brave Man.'

Unlike Sir Robert, who was 'honourably interred' in the churchyard of Falkirk, most of the dead were thrown into a pit dug on the
battlefield. They had been stripped by marauders, and, lying naked
on the hillside, reminded an onlooker of nothing so much as a flock
of sheep. The bodies of the Highlanders were easily recognisable by
a bannock, or other article of food, concealed under the left armpit.

The number of prisoners taken by the Jacobites varies from Lord
George Murray's estimate of 300 to the Chevalier Johnstone's
exaggerated figure of 700. Most of them, being men who had taken
refuge in the surrounding villages, were captured a day or two after
the battle, although about 100, including John Home, fell into
Jacobite hands on the evening of the action. The Lieutenant,
Ensign, and 20 men of the 'Yorkshire Blues' were also taken
prisoner, and Captain Thornton narrowly avoided the same fate by
going into hiding. Among the more remarkable captures were
several Presbyterian ministers, and some of Hawley's hangmen, the
latter being dismissed on giving their paroles, 'as it was Supposed
they would keep them as well as the officers did . . .'. 'By my soul,
Dick', one prisoner was heard to exclaim, 'if Prince Charles goes on
in this way, Prince Frederick will never be King George!'

By accident, the royal army succeeded in taking one prisoner—
MacDonald of Tiendrish, the Major of Keppoch's regiment.
Mistaking Barrel's for Lord John Drummond's regiment, he rushed
up to it exclaiming, 'Why don't ye follow after the dogs and pursue
them?', and was surrounded before he could make his escape. On
his pretending to be a Campbell, Huske ordered him to be shot
instantly—presumably as a spy—but his life was saved by the
intervention of Captain Lord Robert Kerr, who received his arms.
His generous action did the unfortunate Major little good, for he
was afterwards hanged at Carlisle.

According to local tradition, Hawley's first reactions were 'rage
and vexation', and while retreating through Falkirk he is said to
have broken his sword against the Market Cross. By the time he
arrived at Linlithgow this mood had been succeeded by more sober
reflections, and late that evening he wrote in characteristic fashion
to his patron, Cumberland.

> 'Sir, [he began] My heart is broke. I can't say We are quite beat today,
> But our Left is beat, and Their Left is beat. We had enough to beat
> them for we had Two Thousand Men more than They. But suche

scandalous Cowardice I never saw before. The whole second line of
Foot ran away without firing a Shot. Three Squadrons did well; The
others as usual. . . .'

For once, Hawley's self-conceit had been badly shaken, and next
morning a visitor reported that 'he looked most wretchedly; even
worse than Cope did a few hours after his scuffle . . .'.

On the day after the battle the royal army returned to Edinburgh,
'where we were much insulted by the Jacobites', notes Corse. Two
days later Hawley informed the Duke of Newcastle that 'every
wheele is at worke to gett the Engine in motion again. The Foot
recover theyr spiritts, they owne to theyr Officers they all deserve
to be hanged, some Regts: have shooke hands and vowed all to dye
nexte time.' Meanwhile, he had his own ideas of how to restore
discipline, and twelve days after the action sought the Duke's
advice. 'There are fourteen deserters taken, shall they be hanged?
Thirty-one of Hamilton's dragoons are to be hanged for deserting to
the rebels, and thirty-two of the foot to be shot for cowardice.'

Examples were also made of some of the officers, and five,
including Captain Cuningham, were ordered to be put under arrest.
To avoid court-martial 'he . . . opened his Arterys of his Arms', but
recovered, and was sentenced to be cashiered with infamy. This
brutal sentence was later carried out at Montrose:

> 'The line being ordered out under arms, the prisoner was brought
> to the head of the oldest brigade, completely accoutred, when his
> sentence being read, his commission was cancelled, his sword broken
> over his head, his sash cut in pieces and thrown in his face, and lastly,
> the provost-martial's servant giving him a kick on the posteriors,
> turned him out of the line.'

Having driven Hawley back to Edinburgh, and foiled his attempt
to relieve Stirling Castle, the Jacobites were entitled to claim Falkirk
a victory, but instead, the prevailing mood was one of disappointment and recrimination. In a detailed post-mortem of the battle
Lord George lamented the Highlanders' lack of discipline, and the
want of a left-wing commander, while he, in turn, was criticised for
having fought on foot, and for his failure to bring up the right wing
in time.

As to future plans, opinion was divided. Some of the officers were
anxious to follow up Hawley's demoralised army, or even to march
on London. Others argued that, having prevented the enemy from

relieving Stirling Castle, the siege should be continued, especially as the hopeful Mirabel had confidently predicted its surrender within a few days. To have allowed Hawley no breathing-space would unquestionably have been the correct decision, but by what the Chevalier Johnstone calls a 'fatal resolution', it was determined to continue the siege.

> 'The possession of this petty fort was of no essential importance to us; on the contrary, it was of more advantage to us that it should remain in the hands of the enemy, in order to restrain the Highlanders, and prevent them from returning, when they pleased, to their own country, from the fear of being made prisoners in passing this Castle, for they were constantly going home, whenever they got possession of any booty taken from the English, in order to secure it.'

Leaving Lord George Murray with the clan regiments at Falkirk, the Prince returned on the 19th with the rest of the army to Bannock- burn. The previous day a summons of surrender had been sent to Major-General Blakeney, the garrison commander, to which the tough old soldier replied: 'That he had always been looked upon as a man of honour, and that the rebels should find that he would die so.'

Some unusual information about the siege is to be found in Dugald Graham's rhyming history of the Rising, including the fact that the garrison was short of round-shot:

> *Which caus'd them fire with coals and stones,*
> *Or ought was fit for smashing bones . . .*

It was, however, only partly for this reason that Blakeney was careful not to interfere too much with the Jacobites' operations, for knowing they were doomed to fail, he realised that the more time they were allowed to waste over them the better.

Eventually three of the battery's six emplacements were completed, and having mounted one of the 16-pounders and the two 12-pounders, 'Mr. Admirable' gave his assurance that the Castle would be taken within 18 hours of their opening fire on 29th January. What actually happened is described by the Chevalier Johnstone:

> 'M. Mirabelle, with a childish impatience to witness the effects of his battery unmasked it . . . and immediately began a very brisk fire . . . but it was of short duration and produced very little effect on the

batteries of the Castle, which being more elevated than ours, the enemy could see even the buckles of the shoes of our artillerymen. As their fire commanded ours, our guns were immediately dismounted, and in less than half an hour we were obliged to abandon our battery altogether. . . .'

Although Hawley was fortunate in escaping censure for his defeat, it was considered that only one man was capable of restoring the royal army's confidence, and in the early hours of 30th January, the Duke of Cumberland arrived at Edinburgh to take over the command.

Some 4 months younger than the Prince, Cumberland possessed none of his cousin's airs and graces, and was already showing signs of becoming unwieldy. His chief interest was soldiering, and even for a King's son his promotion had been unusually rapid, for barely five years had elapsed since his first appointment as Colonel of the Coldstream and his becoming Captain-General of the Army. Although endowed with no great military ability, he had the complete confidence of his men, and the courage they had shown at the disastrous battle of Fontenoy was a tribute to his powers of leadership.

Since Falkirk the royal army had been joined by the artillery train from Newcastle with a complement of regular gunners. It had also received infantry and cavalry reinforcements consisting of Campbell's Royal Scots Fusiliers (21st), Sempill's (25th), and 3 squadrons of Mark Kerr's Dragoons. With these additions and others on their way, the services of the Glasgow regiment were no longer required, and its officers and men were 'honourably dismissed'. For less honourable reasons the services of Hamilton's and Ligonier's dragoons were also dispensed with, and on the day after the Duke's arrival the royal army marched westwards.

> *Now great Hawley led on, with great Husk at his tail,*
> *And the duke in the centre, this sure cannot fail:*
> *Horse, foot, and dragoons; pell-mell, knock them down;*
> *But, Gadzoons, where are they? Oh, damn them, they're gone.*

They were.

Two days earlier, Lord George Murray and the chiefs of the clan regiments stationed at Falkirk had presented the Prince with an address. This stated that, owing to desertion, they considered the

Highland army in no condition to meet the enemy, who it was known, was to march as soon as the Duke arrived. They therefore advised that an immediate retreat should be made to the Highlands, where the winter could be spent in reducing the Government forts, and an army of 10,000 men could be assembled in the spring. 'The greatest difficulty that occurs to us', the address continued, 'is the saving of the artillery, particularly the heavy cannon; but better some of these were thrown into the River Forth as that your Royal Highness, besides the danger to your own person, should risk the flower of your army . . .'

In reply, Charles argued that a retreat would result in 'nothing but ruin and destruction', and would raise the morale of the enemy and proportionately lower that of the Highland army. It would destroy all hopes of further foreign aid, and, in particular, any prospect of a large-scale French landing. Not only would it result in the loss of the heavy cannon, but by retreating the Highland army would throw away all the advantages it had previously gained. In any case the enemy was no more formidable than it had been a fortnight earlier, and was still smarting from its defeat. Finding, at last, that his objections were in vain, Charles recorded them in a letter to the chiefs. It contained no recriminations, but disclaimed all responsibility for the retreat.

Although it later turned out that the desertions were far less serious than had been supposed, Lord George and the chiefs can hardly be blamed for their action, which was the direct result of the decision to resume the siege of Stirling Castle. For with nothing to do, the Highlanders 'sauntered about all the villages in the neighbourhood of their quarters, and abundance of them had been several days absent from their colours'.

The retreat was begun on the morning of 1st February. The previous day the Duke of Cumberland and most of his army had arrived at Linlithgow, and that evening Lord George Murray and the clan regiments withdrew to Bannockburn, having left a body of horse near Falkirk to keep an eye on the enemy's movements. Late the same night it was agreed that, with the exception of the troops quartered in Stirling, the army would rendezvous near St. Ninians at 9 o'clock the following morning, where a rear-guard would be chosen to be commanded by Lord George Murray. For some unexplained reason, however, orders to this effect were either altered (according to Lord George Murray), or disregarded (according to Kirkconnel), and before daybreak the Highlanders began streaming westwards towards the Fords of Frew. 'Never was their á retreat resembled so much a flight, for their was no where 1000 men together, and the whole army pass'd the river in Small bodies and in great Confusion, leaving Carts & Cannon upon the road behind them.'

On his way to St. Ninians Lord George was startled to hear a loud explosion; he reached the village to find the church in ruins. It had been used by the Jacobites as a store and powder-magazine, and had been accidentally blown up while the powder was being removed, leaving only the tower standing. To add to Lord George's astonishment, he discovered when he arrived at the rendezvous that not a man was in sight, and in no good temper he took the road to Frew.

Having crossed the Forth, the Highland army quartered for the night at Doune and Dunblane, and next day the clan regiments marched on to Crieff, while the rest of the army proceeded to Perth. That evening (2nd February) a council of war was held at Crieff, at which 'there never had been such heats and animosities as at this meeting; however, after a great deal of wrangling and altercation, it was determined that the horse and low country regiments should march towards Inverness, along the coast, while the Prince with the clans, took the Highland road thither'. To Lord George, who 'offered to go the coast road, after others refused it', the decision was probably a welcome one, and on 4th February the two divisions took their separate ways. Meanwhile, following on in pursuit, the royal army left Stirling that same day, and on 6th February Cumberland entered Perth.

6

Prelude to Defeat

THE PRINCE'S division marched by way of Taybridge; at Dalnacardoch it was met by Lord Lewis Gordon with the baggage and artillery from Perth. The train consisted only of eight of the smaller guns, for the larger at Perth had been spiked. After struggling through heavy snow the Prince's and Lord George Murray's divisions reunited about 20th February at Inverness. Two days earlier Lord Loudon and his men had evacuated the town and withdrawn to the Black Isle. The Jacobites, who had taken Fort George after a weak defence, were determined to exploit their success. A strong force under the Earl of Cromarty was sent in pursuit of Loudon, but Cromarty was no soldier, and both Murray and Perth had to take a hand in directing operations. Eventually, when several hundred Government troops had been cornered at Dornoch, the Jacobites forced Loudon to retire with the rest to Skye.

Fort Augustus fell after a week's siege, but Fort William, which was attacked at the insistence of the Camerons and MacDonalds, was a harder nut to crack. Early in the operations Colonel James Grant had been hit by a spent cannon-ball, and under the direction of the fatuous Mirabel little progress was made. In contrast, a raid on the Government outposts in Atholl was brilliantly successful. Lord George, who marched from Inverness with his brigade and was joined by Cluny in Badenoch, made a night attack on the Campbell garrisons, which surrendered after barely firing a shot. When on the point of taking Blair Castle, now occupied by Government forces, he was recalled to Inverness by Sir Thomas Sheridan.

The Prince, who spent most of his time shooting, fishing, and dancing, took no part in any of these proceedings. He seems to have lost his military ardour after the retreat, and when Murray of

Broughton became ill Charles's Irish favourites issued orders without consulting their master—to the great confusion of his affairs.

Realising that he had no chance of overtaking Lord George, Cumberland followed him at a leisurely pace to Aberdeen. His chief task was to raise the morale of his army, and immediately on his arrival there he sent off a detachment to seize a supply of Spanish arms and ammunition at Corgarff Castle in the heart of Jacobite country. He and Hawley lived for six weeks in free quarters, and in spite of stern edicts against plundering, Hawley departed with some hundreds of pounds' worth of his hostess's valuables.

By the middle of March Cumberland was ready to begin operations, and having formed his army into two divisions and a reserve, the first division, commanded by Major-General Bland, marched westwards to Strathbogie, supported by the reserve at Old Meldrum. Here Bland surprised a force of about 1,000 men under John Roy Stewart, which retreated hurriedly to Keith where it, in turn, surprised and captured a small Government advance-guard of Argyll militiamen and Kingston's Horse.

On 8th April the Duke followed with the rest of the army, and three days later linked up with Bland and the reserve at Cullen. On the 12th the army reached the Spey, where it was expected that the Jacobites would attempt to dispute its passage, but to everyone's surprise the river was forded at three places without the least opposition, the only casualties being a dragoon and three women who were drowned.

The Jacobite forces were so dispersed that Perth and his brother, commanding 'the Army of the Spey', were in no position to offer effective resistance. There is, indeed, something not only heroic and pathetic but foredoomed about the last days of the Stuart Cause. The Prince's war-chest was empty, his men without pay; supplies of food and clothing were scarce and disorganised; worst of all, the opinions of the Jacobite leaders were divided. Charles himself remained a blind optimist to the very end, and his inability to face facts served only to widen the breach between him and his long-suffering commander, Lord George Murray.

Cumberland continued his march by way of Elgin and Forres to reach Nairn on the evening of the 14th. So rapid was his approach that Perth and Lord John Drummond had barely time to get clear of the town, and were forced to leave behind a quantity of meal stored there. Falling back along the Inverness road, they rejoined the Prince that evening at Culloden, where he had marched with the rest of the army on hearing of the Duke's advance on Nairn.

The choice of Culloden was not fortuitous. Some days previously Lord George had been ordered to reconnoitre the country lying between the two armies, and had done so in company with Colonel Ker, and Lochiel's uncle, Major Kennedy, who had lately arrived from France. Near Dalcross Castle they had found a stretch of rough and broken ground with the makings of a strong defensive position. O'Sullivan, who was sent by the Prince to view it, considered the ground unsuitable. Instead, he pitched upon a strip of open moorland, a mile to the south-east of Culloden House, where, he maintained, a morass would secure the protection of the Prince's left wing. 'Not one single souldier but would have been against such a ffeeld had their advice been askt', wrote Lord George later. 'A plain moor where regular troups had . . . full use of their Cannon so as to anoy the Highlanders prodigiously before they could possibly make an attack.'

It was on this piece of ground that at dawn on the 15th the Highland army drew up in order of battle. As he had been accused of keeping his brigade out of harm's way at the previous actions, Lord George now insisted on having the Athollmen under his command on the right wing. Thereby he brought to a head 'a violent contestation' that had raged for several days over the vexed question of precedence, and offended MacDonald leaders sought the Prince. 'Clanranald, Keppoch and I', wrote Lochgarry, commander of the Glengarry men, '. . . begged he would give us our former right, but he intreated us for his sake we would not dispute it as he had already agreed to give it to Lord George and his Atholl men.' Knowing that Lord George had shown justifiable resentment at not being consulted about O'Sullivan's choice of ground, there seems little doubt that in giving way to him, Charles intended to avoid further friction.

When they were dismissed the troops dispersed to supplement as best they could their day's ration of a biscuit a-piece. During his march from Aberdeen through Moray, Lord George had done his utmost to secure supplies of meal for the army, but under the Prince's new secretary, John Hay, the Jacobite commissariat had entirely broken down.

'The Misfortune of a total want of provisions was intirly owing to mismanagement. Non of the Principle Officers of the Army were allowed to know any thing with regard to so absolutly and Necessary an article. . . . That there was above ten days provisions in Inverness is certain & a vast deal of Bread had been Bak'd, but wither it was an ill-timed occonomie or that in the Confusion for two days before the battle they had neglected to provide horse to bring out the provisions trow [true] it is there was non to be gott when most wanted. . . . Had provisions been dist[r]ibut as they ought to have been, there would have been no obligation to have given as a reason a presipitat Batle when two thousand more men would have joined in a day or two. . . . But I do not scruple to say that the Prince was made believe by those most in his Confidence that the Highlanders would not fight except they were obliged to do it for want of provisions; these people dreaded a summer campaign in the mountains.'*

One of 'these people' was O'Sullivan, who considered himself quite worn out by the fatigues he had undergone since coming to Scotland.

The supply question was not the only one to weigh heavily on Lord George's mind. He had been able to examine the ground chosen by O'Sullivan even more closely that morning, and was now more than ever convinced that to fight on it would put the Highland army at a fatal disadvantage. Nearer to Culloden than the field he had originally selected at Dalcross, the country south of the Nairn offered the likeliest alternative, and taking advantage of O'Sullivan's absence—he had ridden off to Inverness—Lord George sent Brigadier Stapleton and Colonel Ker to reconnoitre it.

'The Ground which Ld George Murray sent Brigadier Stapleton & Coll. Car to Vew was a very strong Ground, & tho not so inaccessible as some other posts that might be choise at a greater distance, yet it was such as the Highlanders, would have likd very well, & would have thought themselves in a fair way of Victory had the Duke of Cumberland ventur'd to have passt the water of [N]eirn in their Sight, & atact them there; Ld George Murray had formerly vewd that Ground, & upon Brigadier Stapleton & Coll: Cars report he was confirmed in the oppinion that it was infinitely more proper ground for the Highlanders then where they were, or where they fought nixt day.' *

* From an unpublished letter by Lord George Murray preserved at Blair Castle.

Meanwhile, the Prince had become engrossed in another plan. He now walked about the field 'cajoling the different chiefs separately' to fall in with a scheme which he and O'Sullivan had devised for attacking Cumberland's camp at Balblair on the outskirts of Nairn at dawn the following day. They all refused to consider the proposal until they were joined by the expected reinforcements. Perth and his brother also 'expressed their dislike of the measure', and Lord George was 'very sensible of the danger should it miscarry'. Even the Irish judged it 'a desperate attempt'.

The arrival of Keppoch from Lochaber, and a report from Elcho that all was quiet in the enemy's camp, caused Lord George to alter his mind. Almost anything, probably, seemed preferable to him than fighting on that open moor, and at a meeting of officers he put forward his views:

> 'His opinion was that they should march at dusk of that evening so that the Duke should not be apprised of it. He should march about the town of Nairn and attack them in their rear with the right wing of the first line, while the Duke of Perth with the left should attack them in front, and the Prince should support the Duke of Perth's attack with the second line. Everybody agreed to Lord George's opinion. It was only objected to him that, as he did not propose to march from Culloden until the dusk of the evening, and as Culloden was eight miles from Nairn, it was to be feared the army would not accomplish that march before the daylight.'

The attack must be launched before 2 o'clock in the morning, for no one '. . . would have had the madness to have thought of making such an attack except it could be done by Surprise, & in the night time'. Few were let into the secret, and to prevent intelligence reaching the enemy, small parties were sent to patrol the roads, and others ordered to keep fires burning on the moor to mislead them. Two Mackintosh officers and 30 men whose country it was, were also appointed as guides to the first column, and a proportionate number for the second. All these preparations, however, were nearly brought to nothing when about 7 o'clock that evening it was found that a third of the men had gone off in search of food.

> '. . . When the officers who were sent on horseback to bring them back came up with them, they could by no persuasion be induced to return again, giving for answer they were starving; and said to their

officers they might shoot them if they pleased, but they could not go
back till they got meat. . . .

His Royal Highness said that whenever the march began the men
would be all hearty, and those that had gone off would return and
follow . . . he was resolved to attack the enemy without waiting for
those who were to join us. The expression was had he but a thousand
men he would attack. . . .'

Less than 4,500 were at hand to launch this bold assault upon
Cumberland's men, whom O'Sullivan assessed as 18,000 strong, but
who the Prince's Irish favourites assured him would be 'utterly
dispirated and never able to stand an attack'. Lord George's hope
was that as it was the Duke's 25th birthday his men might be 'drunk
as beggars'. The officers who had formerly supported the plan of
attack now, however, declared in the strongest terms for laying it
aside. Much was spoken by them all for not attempting it then.
'But', says Murray, 'His Royal Highness continued bent on the
thing, and gave me orders to march.'

The Highland army marched in two columns, the first being led
by Lord George, and the second by Lord John, with the Prince and
the French troops in the rear. Lord George's plan was to cross the
river two miles short of Nairn, and having marched along the south
bank to avoid the enemy outposts, to recross it a mile farther down-
stream. From the south-east he would then rush in upon the flank
and rear of the royal horse. Meanwhile Lord John's men, heading
straight for the camp, were to turn off to the left shortly before
reaching it, and, having formed line, launch a simultaneous attack
on the enemy foot.

All might have gone well had it been possible to preserve any
semblance of order. But the troops could only make their way
forward in single file, through 'trackless paths, marches, and quag-
mires', where 'men were frequently up to their middles, and horses
in many cases extricated themselves with difficulty'. Although the
first column's speed of advance was no more than two miles an hour,
the heavily-equipped French troops in the rear soon began lagging
behind, and messages arrived from the Prince ordering Lord George
to slacken his pace.

Half-way to Balblair Murray sent back Colonel Ker to warn the
officers not to raise the alarm by the use of fire-arms; but to attack
the tents sword in hand, and 'to strike and push vigorously'

wherever a bulge appeared in the canvas. About the same time he also sent a message to the Prince, requesting that he would form the centre and rear of the second column as they came up, so as to ensure that the attack was made simultaneously and without confusion. In reply he received the astonishing order that he was to attack without waiting for the rest of the troops to arrive.

To Lord George, all hope of the march's succeeding had already vanished. He had set out with considerably fewer than 2,000 men under his command, and many had fallen out while passing through Kilravock wood, 'by faintness for want of food, for it could not have been weariness in a six mile march'. He therefore sent back word by Lochiel that it was useless to continue the march as there was no possibility of his being strong enough to attack.

Charles, however, was quite oblivious to the true state of affairs. He had persuaded himself that, far from being weaker, the army was stronger than when it had left Culloden, and Lochiel returned to the van with positive orders to continue. Soon afterwards Lord George was joined by Lord John Drummond and O'Sullivan, who overtook him at Knockbuie, a mile short of where he had intended to cross the Nairn. They had been ordered forward by the Prince, and Lord John reported that on the way they had seen a gap in the line half a mile in length, and that the men would not come up. Riding up from the rear, Perth confirmed that it was impossible to close the gap, and the van was accordingly ordered to halt.

Forty Life Guards, still smarting from the aspersion that they had floundered into a bog at Falkirk, had asked for permission to attack on foot with the Atholl Brigade. They were eager to engage, even though dawn was almost breaking, but Lord George had no hesitation in declaring that such an attempt 'would be perfect madness'. They would be for two miles in sight of the enemy before they could come at him. To Lochiel and his brother the delay on the part of the rear was inexcusable, and in answer to O'Sullivan's insistence that it was the Prince's wish that the march should be continued, an Atholl officer broke out violently: 'Those that are so much for fighting, why don't they come up with us?' Just then John Hay, the Prince's Secretary, did so, but his expostulations were equally ineffective, for Lord George ignored him. A drum had been heard to beat in the distant camp indicating that Cumberland's men were on the alert, if not already alarmed. 'The day is coming and I have taken my decision', he told his Mackintosh officers, and ordered them to guide his men down to the road leading to Culloden.

The Duke and Lord John rode back to order the second column to face about, but the indignant John Hay was before them. He warned the Prince that 'unless he came to the front and ordered his Lordship to go on nothing would be done', and riding forward Charles came upon the retreating men of the second column. 'Where the devil are the men a-going?' he demanded, and on being told that they had been ordered by Perth to return to Culloden House, he broke out excitedly: 'Where is the Duke? Call him here. I am betrayed! What need have I to give orders when my orders are disobeyed?'

The Duke and O'Sullivan had lost their way in the darkness, and neither they nor Lord George could be found. Aides-de-camp rode about distractedly, demanding 'For God's sake, what has become of his Lordship? The Prince is in the utmost perplexity for want of him.' Eventually, on Perth presenting himself to the Prince, Charles demanded, 'What do you mean by ordering the men to turn about?' to which the Duke replied that Lord George had turned back with the first column three-quarters of an hour before. 'Good God!' cried Charles, 'What can be the matter? What does this mean? We were equal in numbers and could have blown them to the devil. Pray, Perth, can't you call them back yet? Perhaps he has not gone too far?' Perth begged that they might go aside and speak in private, and they were soon joined by Lochiel. The chief was firm. It was now daylight, he said, and it was 'better to march back than go on and attack the Duke, who would be prepared'.

There was nothing for it but to return, and the Prince did his best to encourage his dispirited followers: 'There's no help for it, my lads, march back. We shall meet them later and behave like brave fellows.' In his own mind, however, he was convinced that Lord George was responsible for the failure of the march by having 'put panick in Lochiel'. His favourites did nothing to allay his suspicions, and by the time he reached Culloden he had convinced himself that Murray had deliberately wrecked the plan. He is even said to have ordered some Irish officers 'to watch Lord George's motions, particularly in case of a battle, and they promised the Prince to shoot him if they could find he intended to betray him'.

Dawn had broken when the first column reached Croy. Most of the officers agreed with the necessity of retreating, but both their own and the men's morale had been badly shaken by this abortive and exhausting expedition.

It was indeed a sorry prelude to the impending battle.

7

Culloden

ABOUT 6 O'CLOCK on the morning of Wednesday, 16th April, the main body of the Jacobite army returned to Culloden. The van, although having the greater distance to march, arrived first, for the rear had been delayed by the Lowlanders and the more heavily equipped French auxiliaries.

'Everybody', says Elcho, 'seemed to think of nothing but Sleep', and on returning to Culloden House the principal officers, 'sullen and dejected', lay down to rest, 'some on beds, others on tables, Chairs, & on the floors, for the fatigue and the hunger had been felt as much amongst the officers as Soldiers'. The Prince was among the last to return. On reaching Dalcross Castle at daybreak he had decided to go to Inverness to order the meal stored there to be issued to his starving followers. Between 2,000 and 3,000 of them had gone off in search of food, and during the return march there was much murmuring, not only against the officers, but against the Prince himself. Rightly considering that his royal leader's place was with his army at Culloden, the Duke of Perth galloped after him, and induced him to return. More sensibly Perth and Colonel O'Shea suggested that FitzJames's Horse* should be dispatched to Inverness to bring back provisions, and to this Charles agreed.

The first person whom the Prince encountered on entering Culloden House was Lord George Murray. O'Sullivan says that Charles taxed him with his conduct during the night-march 'without the least anger', whereupon Lord George threw 'all the blame on Lochiel'. The Prince then sent for Lochiel, who stoutly denied Lord George's assertion, declaring that Murray was solely responsible for proposing the retreat. He demanded that he be allowed to tell him

* Part of a regiment in the French service which had landed in Scotland in February.

so to his face in the Prince's presence, but Charles 'wou'd have no other explication, fearing the Ill consequence of it'. A story less in keeping with the characters of the three men it would be hard to imagine, and more plausible is the Chevalier Johnstone's statement that Charles 'on his return to Culloden, enraged against Lord George Murray, publicly declared, that no one in future should command his army but himself'.

The Lord President's well-stocked cellars had been emptied of 60 hogsheads of claret during the Jacobite officers' occupation of his house, and even the Prince had difficulty in getting a little whisky and some bread. Nor could he at once fling himself upon his bed, for d'Éguilles insisted upon a private interview with him, details of which the Marquis set down in a letter to King Louis:

'I requested a quarter of an hour's private audience. There I threw myself at his feet. In vain I represented to him that he was still without half his army; that the great part of those who had returned had no longer their targets—a kind of defensive armour without which they were unable to fight to advantage; that they were all worn out with fatigue by a long march made on the previous night and for two days many of them had not eaten at all for want of bread.

In the end, finding him immovable in the resolve he had taken to fight at any cost, I made my desire yield to my duty. I left him for the first time. I retired in haste to Inverness, there to burn all my papers and there to think over the means of preserving your Majesty that portion of the [French] troops which might survive the action.'

D'Éguilles advised Charles to put the river between himself and his enemies, or to fall back upon Inverness. The first plan meant the abandonment of the meal, artillery, and baggage stored in the town. If, however, the army withdrew there, batteries could be erected on the ruins of Fort George, and, as it was not expected that Cumberland would follow and offer battle that day, the Prince's followers after 24 hours' rest 'would be quite recruited, and altogether new men'. But Charles, wrote the exasperated envoy, 'proud and haughty as he was, badly advised, perhaps even betrayed, forgetting at this moment every other object, could not bring himself to decline battle even for a single day'.

Although no Council was held, some informal discussion took place that morning, for both Keppoch and Lochiel declared themselves strongly against fighting that day. Lord George was also against doing so, and merely refrained from expressing his opinion because, as 'any proposition to postpone fighting was ill-received and was called discouraging to the army', he knew that his advice would not be followed. Charles was again importuned to fall back to the hilly ground beyond the Nairn, but the suggestion roused his instant wrath. 'God damn it!' a royal valet heard him exclaim. 'Are my orders still disobeyed? Fight where you will, gentlemen, the day is not ours.'

It was Walter Stapleton, commander of the Irish picquets, who brought about the fulfilment of Charles's desire to engage the enemy upon the fatal field of Culloden. 'The Scots are always good troops till things come to a crisis', sneered the Brigadier; and just as the Prince's early taunt that Lochiel could return home and read of his fate in the newspapers had led to the chief's raising his clan, so now Stapleton's bitter remark was equally decisive. For Lochiel and the other Highland chiefs there was only one answer to it—to go down in glory fighting against odds on unfavourable ground—for, as he afterwards repeated on several occasions, 'I do not believe that there was a Highlander in the army who would not have run up to the mouth of a cannon in order to refute the odious and undeserved aspersion.'

As was his custom on the march, the Prince lay down without taking off his boots, and tried to snatch a little sleep. He intended that his men should have a good meal on the arrival of supplies from Inverness and hoped that after a day's rest they would be fighting-fit the following morning. With this in view, orders had been given for cattle to be slaughtered there and at Culloden, not only to augment the men's rations but to provide a feast after the victory.

Having been informed of their abortive night-march, Cumberland had no intention of allowing the Highlanders time to recover from it. A Jacobite cavalry patrol clattered in with news that his horse were only four miles off—an unwelcome report confirmed by a Cameron officer, who had fallen asleep in Kilravock wood. At Culloden House there was consternation. Officers, who had eaten nothing all morning and who were sustained only by cups of chocolate provided by a thoughtful servant, hurried off to round up their men, and the Prince, having had an hour's rest, roused himself instantly. Hastening downstairs, he was told by the steward that a roasted side of lamb and two hens were about to be placed on the table, but Charles's mind was on other things: 'Would you have me

28 The Field of Battle at Culloden (From a sketch by Thomas Sandby, 1746)
Reproduced by gracious permission of Her Majesty The Queen

29 Detail from 'An Exact View of the glorious victory . . . at Culloden'. In the background are Inverness and the Moray Firth (From a woodcut of October 1746)

30 Detail from 'A Representation of the Battle on Drunmossie Moor near Culloden'. On horse-back in the left foreground are 'The Young Chevalier' and 'The Chevalier's Man Sulivan' (From a contemporary engraving)

31　Colonel Robert Rich (From a contemporary portrait)

32 'The Effigies of the late Earl of Kilmarnock and the late Lord Balmerino who were beheaded on Tower Hill the 18th of August 1746' (From a contemporary print)

33 (overleaf) 'A Perspective View of the Glorious Battle of Drunmossie Moor . . . 16th April 1746' (From an engraving by G. Williams after J. Hamilton)

Part of Rofs Shire

FIRTH OF

AY   Culloden House   Alterly   Castle Stuart   Ardsyr

A MORASS

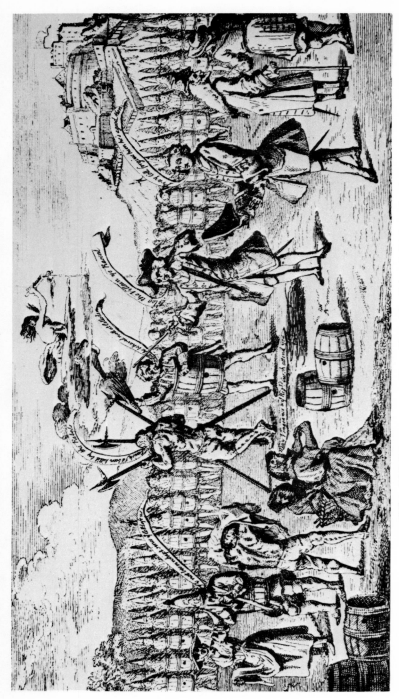

34 'The Old Scourge return'd to Barrels': Colonel Rich maintains discipline in his regiment after their return from Culloden (From a contemporary satirical print)

sit down to dinner when my enemy is so near me?' he exclaimed. 'Eat! I can neither eat nor rest while my poor people are starving.'

It was now too late for the Prince to discuss with his general officers how the field was to be set, or the battle fought. Nor was there time to write fresh orders of the day, and those of the 14th and 15th had to stand.* In the greatest haste the Prince, in company with the Duke of Perth, Lord George Murray, and Lord John Drummond, who commanded respectively the left, right, and centre of his army, mounted and rode off. Drums beat, pipes played, and cannon were fired to recall the Highlanders, causing much confusion among the men, who were half dead with fatigue. '. . . Officers ran about on all sides to rouse them, . . . some were quite exhausted and not able to crawl', wrote Kirkconnel, 'and others asleep in coverts that had not been beat up'. 'Others less exhausted, had slipt off to take some refreshment in the neighbourhood, and designing to take one hour's rest, were afterwards surprised and killed in their beds.' Even the roar of Cumberland's guns had failed to rouse them. At Inverness, where messengers had galloped post-haste, the startled townfolk heard the drums beat to arms and the trumpets of Fitz James's Horse sound the call to boot and saddle. Soon of the Prince's followers there remained there 'only some delicate gentlemen and merchants for whom a battle was too rough exercise'.

The Athollmen and Camerons, the first to return from the night march, had had three hours' sleep—probably in the 'Yellow Hollow' south of Culloden House. They were got ready as quickly as possible, and marched through the parks to the moor, where they were the first troops to reach the field. The Prince accompanied Lochiel's regiment. 'Not the least concern appear'd on his face', wrote the admiring O'Sullivan, ever close to his heels, 'he had yt tallent superiorly in the greatest concern or denger, its then he appears most chearful & harty. . . .' '. . . Here they are comeing, my lades, we'l soon be with them', he told his trusting Highlanders. 'They

* On April 17th Cumberland notified his army that 'the public orders of ye Rebells yesterday was to give no quarters', but no such document was mentioned in any official account of the battle, nor appears to have been seen. Lord George's battle orders printed in a newspaper correspond with four extant copies in his own hand-writing and contain no such suggestion. One is among Cumberland's papers, another belonged to Lord Hardwicke, the Lord Chancellor. But neither man contradicted the calumny refuted by Lords Kilmarnock and Balmerino upon the scaffold.

dont forget, Glads-mur, nor Falkirk, & yu have the same Armes & swords, let me see yours. . . . Il answer this will cut of some heads & arms to-day. Go on my Lads, the day will be ours & we'll want for nothing after.' O'Sullivan, though admitting that his master 'in the bottom had no great hopes', asserts that 'this & the like discourse heartened very much our men . . .'.

The route was rough and in places so steep that there was difficulty in bringing up the guns, and two of the 14 parked at Culloden had to be left behind owing to the scarcity of horses. Only three of the Lord President's had been left in the stables, and of the cavalry horses, which had been in poor condition throughout the winter, the best were on patrol or had been sent to Inverness.

Although the Prince's muster-roll numbered over 8,000 men, only some 7,000 of them were then in the vicinity of Culloden. The Mackenzies, MacGregors, Mackinnons, and Barisdale's MacDonalds were in the North with Lord Cromarty. Lochiel's men had returned from the unsuccessful siege of Fort William on 14th April, and Keppoch's the following afternoon. Both regiments were at half the strength they had been at Falkirk. Cluny's 300 clansmen, who had been in Badenoch, were thought to be on their way to Culloden, and Charles Fraser, the younger of Inverallochy, now arrived with 300 men, and reported that a second Fraser regiment led by the young Master of Lovat was on the march to Inverness.

In Murray of Broughton's absence due to illness, the septua-genarian Sir Thomas Sheridan, who had suffered three slight strokes before embarking on the expedition, had taken his place as military secretary. He was not a success, and thanks to his muddled forget-fulness the Prince's leading officers had the utmost difficulty in discovering where the old man had posted certain units, and in recalling them in time for the forthcoming battle.

On the alarm being raised there were no more than 1,000 men ready to take the field. For this reason they drew up 'further back than they had done the day before & on a much less advantageous spot of ground', wrote John Cameron, who was among the first to reach it. One of its more obvious disadvantages was that, unlike the former position, there was no morass to protect the Jacobite left wing; all that could be said in favour of it was that, being half a mile farther west, Cumberland would have so much farther to march. Conversely, the Prince could be joined more quickly by those of his followers who had gone to Inverness or to the neighbouring villages, most of which lay to the west of Culloden.

On gaining the moor the Prince was so anxious to see his army 'immediately formed in order of battle' that he curtly refused Lord George's request for 'a little time to view the ground'. The unfortunate result of this was that nobody seems to have been aware of the boggy nature of the slight hollow which the Highlanders would have to cross in the event of their charging the enemy, as in the two previous engagements.

O'Sullivan, like the Prince, was obsessed with the idea that Cumberland was nearer at hand than was actually the case. Although admitting the time ill-chosen, he had been bled and purged a few days previously, and was still in his own eyes so much of an invalid that Lord George was later to remark sarcastically that he had fought the battle in his night-cap. For these reasons he now decided to save himself time and trouble by leaving the Highlanders' order of battle unchanged—thus denying the place of honour on the right to the Camerons, whose turn it was to occupy it in succession to the Atholl Brigade, who had held it the previous day. To Lord George's expostulations the Irishman replied with his customary vagueness that there had been no battle the day before, and that in any case it was no time to change the order of battle in the enemy's presence. Still protesting, Lord George, on the Prince's insistence, led up his men. 'Gad, Sr', he remarked to O'Sullivan, 'it is very hard that my Regimt must have the right two days running', and he went on to complain that the ground where it was to be posted had not been reconnoitred. To this the Adjutant-General made the unconvincing reply that it was as good a position as could be desired, and he proceeded to enlarge on its supposed advantages.

To Lord George, O'Sullivan's vapourings merely confirmed his unfitness for his post. During his twenty years' service in the French army the Adjutant-General had been chiefly employed on baggage-master's duties, and at Prestonpans and Falkirk had had no opportunity of demonstrating his tactical knowledge. But at Culloden he had 'forty-eight hours to display his skill, and did it accordingly', wrote Lord George. 'I am certain that neither the Scots officers or one single man of all the Highlanders would have agreed to it had their advice been asked, for there never could be more improper ground for Highlanders.'

An example of such 'improper ground' was the position to which the Atholl Brigade had been assigned, which was behind the western wall of an enclosed and partially cultivated part of the moor extending south to the river Nairn, known as Culloden Parks. Since this dry-stone wall, directly in front of his men, would have made it impossible for them to charge, Lord George at first proposed to demolish part of it. He was, however, overruled, for 'as such a movement would have broken the line the officers about him considered the attempt would be dangerous, and he therefore did not make it'.

Nevertheless, there would have been time to have done so, and time also, Lord Elcho thought, to have crossed the Nairn to the hilly country beyond it. But the die was cast, the decision made, and in choosing to fight on the flat, bare stretch of moorland the Prince, with fatal surety, laid the foundations of his defeat. He could not have given a better present to Cumberland, who had celebrated his birthday the previous day, and whose force of almost 9,000 men—better armed, trained and disciplined—outnumbered his own by nearly two to one.

Reveille had been sounded at 4 o'clock that morning at Cumberland's camp at Balblair, which lay about a mile to the southwest of Nairn. The day before, to mark his 25th birthday, he had supplied his men with bread, cheese, and brandy at his own expense, and had made them a short speech. 'My brave boys', he said, 'we have but one march more and all our labour will be at an end. Sit down at your tent doors, and be alert to take your arms.' He then withdrew to his quarters, where he called his officers together and urged them to do all they could to encourage the men, who were to meet the enemy next day. 'Lights out' was sounded at 10 p.m., and the men were ordered to sleep with their arms beside them. Cumberland slept in his clothes and boots.

News of the failure of the Jacobites' night attack was brought in by spies next morning as the royal army was preparing for the march.

'It was a very cold rainy Morning, [wrote Alexander Taylor, of the Royal], and nothing to buy to comfort us. But we had the Ammunition loaf, thank God; but not a Dram of Brandy or Spirits had you given a Crown for a Gill, nor nothing but the Loaf and Water. We also had great difficulty in keeping the Locks of our Firelocks dry; which was very necessary, for the Day was stormy and the Rain violent.'

On coming from his quarters Cumberland was both surprised and

pleased to find that his whole army had been drawn up in regimental
order in no more than two minutes. He was still more pleased to
hear of the failure of the night march, and ordered every man to be
given a tot of brandy, and a ration of biscuit and cheese. Tents were
struck at 5 o'clock, and a quarter of an hour later the royal army
marched off in three infantry columns of five regiments each. The
artillery and baggage followed the first column on the right, the
cavalry forming a fourth column on the left. Recruits and the women
of the regiment marched with the bat-horses, between the general
officers' baggage and the wheel-baggage of the army. Led by the
Quartermaster-General, the advance-guard consisted of part of
Cumberland's Highlanders and 40 of the Duke of Kingston's Light
Horse, the newly-raised regiment which had helped in the pursuit of
the Highland army during its retreat from Derby, and more recently
had been the first to cross the Spey. Like Charles's men, the Duke's
Highlanders seem to have lived up to the nickname of 'hill-skippers',
so often given them by Lowlanders:

> With Kingston's Horse as spies and van,
> From hill to hill they skipt and ran,

keeping two miles ahead, but somewhat to the south of the main
body.

This marched by Kildrummie Moss, the Loch of the Clans, Loch
Flemington, and to the north of Dalcross Castle. The Prince's horse
were in so poor a state that no further patrols had been sent out, and
Cumberland, surprised at their absence, suspected an ambush,
against which he is said to have been warned. He therefore sent off a
cavalry screen in the direction of Kilravock wood, but soon afterwards some 'honest people', as the Whigs termed these informers,
came hurrying eastwards to report that the Highland army appeared
to be taking up position on the moor about a mile south of Culloden
House.

This information was confirmed by Captain Colin Campbell
of Ballimore, whose company of Loudon's Highlanders had been
ordered to reconnoitre Kilravock wood. From there he had seen the
Highland army marching out from the Culloden enclosures, and he
at once galloped back to report. Three companies of the Argyll
Militia and a small squadron of Kerr's Dragoons were accordingly
ordered to join him and continue the advance. 'Thus we moved till

we . . . discovered the rebels formed in a moor', recorded Captain Duncan Campbell of the Glenorchy company. 'We then made a halt and sent notice to Colonel Campbell. In a little time the Duke with all the general officers came up and viewed the enemy, after which they returned. . . . We were ordered to move on. When the enemy was formed we advanced. . . . The Dragoons followed us.'

Still keeping to the southward, and slightly ahead of the main body, the Campbells turned up a short hollow lane, which led from the river to Urchal, a clachan of three houses. Here they found themselves confronted by 'a high enclosure that extended a great way to the right, and quite to the Water of Earn [Nairn] on the left. From this place', continues Captain Campbell, 'we sent to acquaint General Bland that the Horse could go no further. He came up to the ground and ordered us to pull down the wall, which was done so that the squadron could march abreast.' This wall formed the eastern boundary of the Culloden parks, the breach made in it being immediately to the north of the wall dividing the upper park from the lower.

Meanwhile Cumberland and the main body of the royal army had turned off the old moor road which ran along the eastern end of the 'Yellow Hollow'. He thus avoided this tract of boggy ground, but even so some of his men were forced to splash their way knee-deep through morasses, for, as one of them wrote disgustedly, it was 'very moorish country'. Progress was slow, and there was a succession of heavy showers which made it difficult for the troops to keep their firelocks dry.

As the march proceeded it inclined towards the south, for the Highland army had moved farther in that direction than had been expected, and could now be seen clustered 'behind some old walls and huts' at the summit of a low hill. To one of Cumberland's soldiers it seemed to be 'artfully' posted, but so small were its numbers in comparison with the reports of spies that there must still have appeared a possibility that the rest of the army was being held in readiness to launch an attack from some other quarter.

By this time—it was about 11 o'clock—the opposing armies were in full view of each other, some 2½ miles apart, and having continued his march for another half-mile, Cumberland halted, and drew up in order of battle.

The three columns had been led by the Royal, Price's and Munro's regiments, followed by Cholmondeley's, Campbell's (Royal Scots

Fusiliers), and Barrel's. On forming, the three latter regiments now came up on the left of the three former, to make a front line of six battalions. A second line, with the same number of regiments, was formed in a similar manner, although one of them—Howard's— seems later to have fallen back to the third line, or reserve, which included the remaining three battalions. On each flank, and slightly in advance of the reserve were the rest of the Highlanders, and Kingston's Horse, the latter consisting of two squadrons. The baggage and the dragoons remained on the left, excepting for 60 of Cobham's troopers, who were sent to reconnoitre the country in the direction of Culloden House. It is probable that some of the guns intended for the right were also moved over to that wing at this time.

Cumberland was pleased to find that these movements 'were performed without the least confusion', but he would not permit his men to dine before the battle. They would fight better on empty bellies, he said, apart from its being a bad omen—'remember what a dessert they got to their dinner at Falkirk!' As for himself, he would not dine until his work was done. Although the General Orders of the day had been read at the head of every regiment before the march began, and each colonel had received his instructions in writing, the Commander-in-Chief now rode along the newly-formed lines, addressing every battalion, and almost every company. 'Depend, my lads, on your bayonets', he said. 'Let them mingle with you; let them know the men they have to deal with.'

He also delivered a short speech:

'Gentlemen and Fellow-Soldiers,
    I have but little Time to address myself to you; but I think proper to acquaint you, That you are instantly to engage in the Defence of your King and Country, your Religion, your Liberties, and Proper- ties; and thro' the Justice of your Cause, I make no Doubt of leading you on to certain Victory. Stand but firm, and your Enemies will soon fly before you. But if there be any among you, who through Timidity, are diffident of their Courage or Behaviour, which I have not the least Reason to suspect, or any others, who through Conscience or Inclination cannot be zealous or alert in performing their Duty; it is my Desire, that all such would immediately retire: and I further declare, that they shall have my free Pardon for so doing for I had much rather be at the Head of One Thousand brave and resolute

Men, than Ten Thousand amongst whom there are some who by
cowardice or Misbehaviour, may dispirit or disorder the Troops, and
so bring Dishonour and Disgrace on any Army under my Command.'

Although his words could reach only a small audience—they were
jotted down by an officer who heard them—the fact that he felt it
necessary to express himself in such terms betrayed Cumberland's
anxiety over the issue of the battle. He had done his utmost to restore
his men's confidence; how far he had succeeded in doing so had still
to be proved.

The army then resumed its march with flying colours, to the
beating of drums and the sound of the Campbell pipes. The men
were ordered to march with 'arms secured and Bayonets fixed, (a
very uneasy way of marching)'; thought Alexander Taylor of the
Royal, and the youthful Colonel Joseph Yorke, aide-de-camp to the
Duke, gave a clear description of what followed:

> 'We marched forward so formed towards the rebels. As we drew
> near I could observe that this manoeuvre of ours had caused a good
> deal of confusion among them and they seemed to incline more
> towards the Water of Nairn. This inclination of theirs being observed,
> our left continued stretching out that way too, and at the same time
> Lt.-General Hawley and Major-General Bland with five squadrons of
> Dragoons unperceived by them crept along the side of the descent to
> the river in order to fall upon their flank if they should according to
> custom endeavour to gain ours.'

At this stage, however, the dragoons cannot have moved so far,
for in plans of the battle they are depicted as having been close to the
army's left flank when it finally halted—probably just inside the
Leanach enclosures. Serving that day with Cobham's was James Ray
of Whitehaven, a mounted volunteer. He had seen a man standing
beside the Leanach house, and thinking that it might be occupied
by the enemy he asked permission to reconnoitre it. The man—the
only person to remain in this dangerous neighbourhood—seemed to
be a friend of the Government, and gave Ray what information he
could about the movements of the Jacobites. From Leanach the
volunteer had 'a good view' of them, noting in particular that they
were closing in towards the park wall on their right; 'as if they
intended to bring their greatest strength there . . .'. He also made a
careful examination of the ground, which immediately to the west
of Leanach appeared to be soft and marshy, but within the Culloden

parks seemed dry and firm. To Hawley, who commanded the cavalry on the left, Ray's information was most valuable, for once the necessary breaches had been made in the east and west walls there was nothing to prevent the dragoons from passing through the parkland to the open moor behind the Highland lines.

From Culloden House Ker of Graden, the best scout in the Highland army, had been sent on reconnaissance, and 'money was given to the MacIntoshes that knew the roads' to bring in what information they could. They had returned before the royal army had come into view, and their reports and the sight of Cumberland's men, now in full march towards them, did little to raise the spirits of the Prince's unfortunate followers. They had hoped that owing to the bad weather the Duke would postpone his march, and then—as vainly—that the rain would render his muskets useless. Later, on his halting to form order of battle, it was at first supposed that he intended to encamp, but as the Chevalier Johnstone wrote, 'he must have been blind in the extreme to have delayed attacking us instantly in the deplorable situation in which we were . . .'.

To the more experienced the situation seemed hopeless. A French officer told the Prince 'he feared the day already lost for he had never seen men advance in so cool and regular a manner'. Even O'Sullivan, though endeavouring to keep up the best countenance he could, had to admit that the enemy appeared 'in every good order', and Lord George Murray and Lord Kilmarnock were equally pessimistic. 'We are putting an end to a bad affair' was the former's reply to Lord Elcho, who asked him what he thought would be the outcome of the battle. Nor could the Prince's blind optimism any longer withstand the facts now facing him, and for the first time he 'began to consider his situation desperate'.

Amid the roll of Cumberland's 225 kettle-drums could be heard the faint skirling of the Campbell pipes. Lochiel's quick eye had detected some of the clan, accompanied by a party of dragoons, making towards the river, and he immediately sent an aide-de-camp to Lord George with this information. About 400 yards from where Murray stood the land fell so sharply that the lower of the Lord President's parks could not be seen. From the first he had realised that there was every prospect of the Jacobite right wing being taken in flank and rear if Cumberland's cavalry advanced over this stretch of dead ground. He now said so in forthright fashion to

O'Sullivan, by whom the Prince, although well aware of their mutual dislike, still persisted in sending his orders.

He also told the Adjutant-General that he had committed an irretrievable error in allowing the enemy 'so fair a field for their horse and cannon'. In reply O'Sullivan made an unconvincing attempt to be reassuring.

> 'Never fear yt My Ld', he said, 'they cant come between yu & the river, unlesse they break down the walls of those two parks, yt are between yu & them. . . . My advise wou'd be, as all their horse is at their left, yt we shou'd make a breach in this wall, & set in this park, Stony Wood & the other Regimt yt is in Colloum behind yu, who will take their horse in flank. . . . If the horse is taken in flanck, with such a wall as this between them, & those yt fires on 'em, Il answer they'l break. If they are once broak, the foot will not stand, besides my Ld, if yu march to the enemy, as yu have no other party [course] to take, for I suppose yu dont pretend to measure yr fire with the English troops; in case yu are repuls'd, those same troops yt you'l set in the Park will protect your retrait. I'd do more My Ld. I'd set fifty men in each of those houses . . . get the walls pierc'd, what we call crenelle, & yt will assure yr retraite altogether, in case of misfortune.'

These buildings may have been the huts shown on some plans near the north-east angle of the wall, or the two, about the middle of the upper park, known as the 'park houses'. In any case O'Sullivan's futile optimism and his patronising 'professional' tone can have done little to relieve Lord George's anxiety. To be rid of him Murray sent him with Ker of Graden and John Roy Stewart to reconnoitre what lay between the wall where they had been standing and the river, flowing half a mile away, on the far side of the lower park. Riding along the side of the west wall they entered the upper park by a gate leading to the park houses. The park consisted mainly of heather with a few arable patches, and for some distance along the brow of the hill the ground was level, but farther east it sloped downwards towards a hollow containing the spring now known as 'The Well of the Dead'. Beyond that again, but still some considerable distance away, Cumberland's army could be seen advancing across the open moor, and further investigations revealed the unpleasant fact that the Campbells and their cavalry escort were on the far side of the east park wall near the river.

On returning to report to Lord George the two colonels con-
curred in O'Sullivan's view that there was no threat to the Jacobite
right wing from this quarter. Their optimism seems the more
extraordinary, since both were men of experience—Graden having
seen service in the Spanish army, and Stewart in the British and
French. According to Graden the banks of the river were too high
for cavalry to come that way, while O'Sullivan asserted that such a
movement was impossible 'without first throwing down the walls'.
It does not seem to have occurred to him that this would be no
insuperable difficulty.

The Atholl and Cameron officers all feared an outflanking movement, and O'Sullivan's bland assurances carried little weight.

> 'Some proposed lining the park wall. The Duke of Perth, who had
> come over from the left, was of that opinion. But Lord George
> thinking otherwise ordered Lord Ogilvy's Regiment to cover the
> flank, and the two battalions were posted facing outwards which
> covered the right of the lines, to observe the motions of the enemy if
> they should make an attempt that way.'

Lord George had insufficient men to waste them in manning
houses which could be easily by-passed, and finding himself ignored,
O'Sullivan went off to report matters to the Prince. Charles, with a
great show of outward confidence, was riding about encouraging
his troops. He was mounted on a fine horse presented to him by
Mr. Dunbar of Thunderton, and was armed with a pair of silver-
mounted pistols and a French-made leather targe embossed with a
silver head of Medusa. He reminded them of how much depended
upon their making a bold stroke, and having done all he could 'to
set them in Sperits', he withdrew to a 'slight eminence' behind the
gap in the centre of the second line.

His hopes now rose that Cumberland's cavalry and artillery would
be impeded by the marshy ground, for when about 600 yards from
the Jacobite front line, the men of Wolfe's regiment on the extreme
left of the Duke's second line were ankle-deep in water. There was
also trouble on the royal right where Robert Fraser, a former servant
of Lord Lovat, who was acting as a guide, cunningly 'contrived that
the cannon should be conveyed rather too far to the right . . . where
one was seen to sink in an unsuspected patch of hollow swampy
ground'. Cumberland, whose eye was on everything, immediately

ordered additional horses to its assistance, and men were seen unslinging their muskets and hurrying to help in extricating it.

With his dragoons on the left and his light horse in rear, Cumberland's right wing was now temporarily uncovered, and the eager young Prince decided that the time had come to launch a spirited attack on him. Everything seemed to favour this course of action, and he afterwards told John Roy Stewart that had Lord George Murray agreed to it, he 'would have driven the enemy's front line into the rear'. It was therefore probably now, rather than later—O'Sullivan's timing of events is far from reliable—that the Prince sent the Adjutant-General with a message to Lord George 'to march on directly upon the enemy ... now is the time to have troops in the Park yt will take the horse in flanck when yu are marching upon them'.

It is not unlikely that Lord George found the Prince's order—or his bearer's version of it—as difficult to understand as do readers of O'Sullivan's 'Narrative', and he answered the Irishman 'no more then if he spook to a Stone ...'. Various reasons are given for Lord George's refusal to comply with the Prince's instructions. Kirkconnel states that because of the protection afforded by the walls on his right he thought it better to await Cumberland's advance; McNab of Inishewen's explanation was that only '1700 men had as yet come up the hill to take up position in the front line'. Inishewen's premise was probably the more correct, for, on O'Sullivan's own showing, all the regiments forming the front line were not then drawn up, and an eye-witness observed that 'the men were standing in clusters'. To have issued such an order under these conditions lends weight to Lord Elcho's remark that figures meant nothing to the Prince.

Meanwhile, on Cumberland's right the cannon had been hauled clear of the morass, with its carriage slightly damaged, and he continued his advance. His men made no response to the Highlanders' wild shouts, and there was something menacing about the royal army's slow deliberate approach. 'It resembled', wrote an English Jacobite, 'a deep and sullen river while the Prince's army might be compared to a streamlet running among stones, whose noise sufficiently showed its shallowness.'

O'Sullivan, intent all morning on issuing instructions to Lord George—who had irritably asked him if he commanded the army—

only recollected his own duties as Adjutant-General when the enemy was just out of cannon-shot. He then began to make feverish attempts to 'rightify' the Jacobite front line, in which, as Cumberland's officers were pleased to observe, there was 'a deal of confusion'. He soon discovered, however, that in deciding to set the field in the same order as on the 15th, he had increased rather than diminished his difficulties. For although Lochiel, in his usual generous fashion, had ceded his rights that day to the Athollmen, the MacDonalds remained unpacified, and 'in general were far from satisfied with the complaisance of their commanders'. Sir John MacDonald, Clanranald's mischief-making old cousin, had done his work only too well; and alarmed by mutterings as he rode with them to the moor, he sent Captain Felix O'Neil to report 'to Sheridan and the Prince, if he thought fit, that it was most important not to offend the clans'.

It is probable that the Athollmen, known as 'the Flower of the Army', were at greater strength than any other clan regiment, for they had recently received reinforcements, and had suffered no desertions, owing to Atholl being under enemy occupation. On the other hand, many of Clanranald's and Glengarry's men had left their colours following the accidental shooting of Glengarry's son at Falkirk by a Clanranald clansman, who on the Glengarry men's insistence had forfeited his life. So much was this resented by Clanranald's followers that he had with him 'but a handful of his people'. Many of Keppoch's followers had remained in Lochaber after the siege of Fort William had been raised, while Barisdale's MacDonalds, who had served with his regiment, were with Cromarty in the North. The number of MacDonalds present at Culloden, was, in fact, 'insignificant'.

If Inishewen's estimate is correct, the MacDonalds must have been late in arriving on the field. They made an ineffectual attempt to claim the coveted post on the right, and then drew up near the centre of the line. Finally they moved so far to the left that Glengarry's regiment—on the extreme left—was posted near the southeast corner of the wall surrounding the Culloden enclosures. This would have mattered little had it not been for two important considerations. The first of these was that this enclosure wall and the park wall on the Jacobite right were not more than 700 yards apart; in consequence there was insufficient room between them for the front-line regiments to draw up if at full strength. The second was the fact that, contrary to O'Sullivan's assertion, the enclosure wall ended considerably to the west of where the park wall began, with the result that, in taking up their position, the MacDonalds threw the front line askew—a circumstance noted by both Kirkconnel and Graden.

The awkwardness of this situation became still more apparent on Lord George Murray ordering the Atholl Brigade to move from behind the west park wall on to the moor. In order to give his men an unobstructed front he had to lead them well clear not only of the Jacobite right-wing battery but of a half-ruinous turf dyke, which projected from the north side of the Leanach enclosures. The result was to bring them almost 200 yards nearer the centre of the Jacobite position, and considerably farther forward. As this, in turn, would obviously lead to overcrowding, he was obliged to instruct the right-wing regiments to re-form in six, instead of three ranks to allow sufficient space for those posted in the centre and on the left. A further effect of Lord George's movement was to throw the Jacobite front line still more askew, a circumstance which he probably considered unimportant, as it could easily be rectified by the Duke of Perth bringing forward the left wing.

Posted in front of the Glengarry men, whose murmuring filled him with foreboding, the tactful and popular Duke found it impossible to prevail on the MacDonalds to advance. With no bog to protect their flank, as on the previous day, they showed an understandable reluctance to leave the shelter of the enclosure wall; but although the only hope of victory was a simultaneous attack by the whole of the Jacobite front line, the Duke received no help from O'Sullivan. Hearing a cry of 'Close, close!', and unable to imagine what it meant, the Adjutant-General galloped back along the front of the line, finding in it 'intervals, yt he had not seen before'. On blaming Murray for all that had gone wrong, Lord George maintained his stony silence, and the distracted O'Sullivan hurried off to the second line, 'for there was no time to be lost, to fill up the vecansy yt was left (by Ld Georges changemt) with the Duke of Perth's & Strathallan's Regiment'.

O'Sullivan's writings reveal a thoroughly muddled mind, and in this instance it was not Viscount Strathallan's troopers whom he now ordered to move up from the second line with the Duke of

Perth's men, but Gordon of Glenbucket's regiment. Neither of these units could be considered reliable. Being now too frail for active service, old John Gordon had turned over the command of his regiment to his two ineffective sons, one of whom was nearly blind. It had been brought up to strength by numbers of 'pressed men' from Strathbogie. All were without swords, and had not taken part in the previous battles. As for Perth's regiment, half of it consisted of Lowlanders, who at Prestonpans are described as having 'stood stock-still like oxen'.

The Prince complained that the clansmen were slow in assembling, but the situation had been bedevilled by his having sent the colonels of some of the regiments to Inverness to fetch rations for their men. They had returned with FitzJames's Horse, and with them had come a band of sightseers, some carrying picnic baskets, and eager not to miss the excitements of the day. Having been employed on hard and continuous duty for several days and nights, a number of the Jacobite horse were in such a broken-down state that they had not yet returned after taking part in the night-march. Robert Strange and some fellow Life Guards, 'too weary to get back along the road, had slept in an outhouse with their horses fastened to their ankles'. Luckily for them the woman of the house had awakened them in time, and they had managed to hurry back to their lines ahead of the oncoming enemy. For others there was less excuse. Instead of drawing up on the moor 300 strong the Farquharsons found themselves a company short. It was afterwards discovered that the men had stopped for refreshment at a farm and were dancing to their captain's fiddling when the sound of firing announced that the fighting had begun.

The two armies were now only some 500 yards apart. They were well within range of each other's artillery, and having halted, the Duke ordered forward his ten 3-pounders. They were brought up in pairs through the intervals between the six front-line regiments and were drawn up in line some distance in advance of them. His six coehorn mortars, in two batteries of three, were posted slightly in advance of the two regiments on the right and left wings of his second line. Unlike the Duke's artillery, the Prince's 12 cannon were a mixed collection, including 1½-pounders, 3-pounders, and 4-pounders, but unfortunately, there seems to be no record showing the number of each calibre. They were divided into three 4-gun

batteries, which were sited in the centre and on the wings of the
Jacobite front line, and slightly in advance of it. An old print of the
battle shows the guns protected by *gabions*—large cylindrical wicker
baskets filled with earth.

The Duke's men were hardly less weary than the Prince's, for they
had marched 10 miles that morning—the same distance as the
Jacobite rear-guard. Yet all were impatient to attack the enemy and
avenge past defeats by men they thought traitors for taking up arms
while Britain was at war with France. Recalled from their comfortable
winter quarters in Flanders to Wade's water-logged camp at Newcastle, their grudge had become a personal one during their long and
fatiguing march through frost-bound Scotland. The towns were
small, and billets scarce and often squalid; some of the men had not
taken their clothes off for six weeks; yet in spite of these and other
discomforts the army had been well supplied with provisions from
the fleet of victuallers that accompanied it along the coast. This had
given the rank and file a vast confidence in their 'dear Bill . . . but
for whom we should have starved', one soldier wrote home. A rebel
threat that the Duke would be 'cut small as herbs for the pot', and
an unconfirmed rumour that a 'No quarter' order had been found
on a recently captured prisoner, can have done little to soften their
feelings towards the Jacobites.

Many suggestions had been made in public journals 'for putting
the weapons of the regular troops upon a par with those of the
insurgents', and in Army circles considerable thought had been
given to the same subject. Hawley, as already mentioned, had
emphasised the importance of fire-power in breaking the Highlanders' attack, but his theoretically 'sure way to demolish them'
had proved anything but certain in practice. Since then a new method
of bayonet-fighting, said to have been evolved by Barrel's officers,
had been introduced by Cumberland. This laid down that the soldier,
instead of attacking the Highlander directly facing him, and thus
giving him a chance to deflect the thrust with his targe, should
engage the Highlander next on the right, whose upraised sword-arm
left his right side temporarily exposed. The practical value of this
new drill is difficult to assess, but during the royal army's halt at
Aberdeen it had been assiduously practised and had done much
to increase the men's confidence.

Jacobite officers, viewing the opposing army through their perspective glasses, admitted that it occupied 'advantageous ground', and 'made a very good appearance', while Cumberland's were well satisfied by its 'prudent disposition', for which the Duke's secretary, Sir Everard Fawkener, gave him the entire credit. Each second-line regiment was posted to cover the interval between the two first-line regiments in front of it, so that, as one enthusiastic commentator remarked: 'If one column failed, a second supported; and if that failed, a third was ready. The rebels could no way take two pieces of cannon, but a third must play directly upon them, nor break one regiment, but two were ready to supply their place.'

The Duke's orderly, disciplined lines were in striking contrast to the Prince's, now brought to some sort of 'confused form'. Apart from its disorganisation and shortage of numbers, the morale of the Highland army had never been lower, and this depression is reflected in every written account left by the Jacobite officers. 'Bad signs had been multiplying throughout the morning', and 'a visable damp and dejection had spread among the troops'. 'They were not the clans that had fought with such verve and vigour at Prestonpans and Falkirk'; 'quite different was their appearance this day from what it had been the day before'—are some of their comments.

As 'Mr. O'Sullivan drew up the army in line of battle I cannot justly tell in what order they were drawn up', Lord George Murray later told a friend. He had then estimated 'there was not above 3000 in the field, and those not in the best order. . . . At the time the Prince was in the rear of all, ordering some men to replace some others that had been sent from the second line to the left of the first', and these replacements must have been Lord Kilmarnock's Foot Guards, the only remaining infantry regiment in the much-depleted Highland reserve. 'The English were drawn up in three lines, but we had much difficulty in forming two', wrote the Chevalier Johnstone, and in similarly comparing the opposing armies Lord Elcho remarks that, unlike Cumberland's second line, which was longer than the first, 'the Prince had no continued second line, but only three bodies to cover the right, centre and left of the first line'. Not one of them was over 200 strong, and the three other regiments, which formed the wings of the second line, were posted so far to the rear that they could hardly be considered part of it—a circumstance which may have been responsible for Henderson's mistake in asserting that the Prince's second line was half a mile behind the first. It was commanded by Brigadier Stapleton, and not —as is sometimes stated—by Colonel John Roy Stewart, whose regiment was in the front line.

At the beginning of the action the Jacobite front-line regiments were posted, from left to right, in the following order: the Clan Donald regiments, consisting of Glengarry's, Keppoch's, and Clanranald's; Perth's, Glenbucket's and John Roy Stewart's; and those of the Farquharsons, MacLeans and MacLachlans, Mackintoshes, Frasers, Stewarts of Appin, Camerons, and the three battalions of the Atholl Brigade. In all they numbered about 3,000 men.

In the same order, the second line consisted of the Irish picquets, Lord John Drummond's regiment (Royal Scots), the remaining battalion of Lord Lewis Gordon's, and two of Lord Ogilvy's guarding the wall. It also included the 40 men of Lord Kilmarnock's Foot Guards, brought forward from the reserve, although their exact position is uncertain. Guarding the right flank were Lord Elcho's troop of Life Guards and that of FitzJames's horse, the last-named having just returned from Inverness.

Stationed a short distance in rear of the centre of the second line was the Prince with the reserve—'so called because there was no other', wrote Kirkconnel bitterly—which consisted of Lord Balmerino's 16 Life Guards, and a slightly larger number of hussars.

In addition to these units were the two small regiments commanded by Moir of Stoneywood and Sir Alexander Bannerman, which occupied an isolated position well in rear of the left of the second line. Similarly detached, but more effectively posted, was Gordon of Avuchie's regiment, which was stationed near the northwest corner of the Culloden park wall.

Shortly after 1 o'clock the twenty-one-year-old Lord Bury, son of the Earl of Albemarle, who commanded Cumberland's front line, rode out into the no-man's land separating the two armies. He had been sent forward with a small party to reconnoitre 'what . . . appeared like a battery behind several old walls'—evidently those to the north of Leanach. Bury had had an unpleasant experience that morning. Pretending to give himself up as a prisoner, a Highlander, while being led to the rear, had seized a soldier's musket and discharged it at the dandified young officer, whose blue and scarlet coat he had mistaken for the Duke's. The would-be assassin had been immediately shot dead, and Bury was quite unperturbed by his narrow escape.

He made his reconnaissance of what turned out to be a non-existent battery equally coolly, riding within 100 yards of the Highland right wing. Breaking its ominous silence the royal army raised a cheer, and although 'faint with hunger, and ready to drop down with fatigue', the Highlanders returned it with 'alacrity and spirit'. Pipes skirled and bonnets were tossed in the air.

Bury had barely returned to the royal army's lines when the action began. The opening shots were fired by the four-gun battery in the Jacobite centre. Orders had been given to the Prince's gunners to aim to the rear of the enemy's front line, where it was thought that Cumberland was stationed, and one of the few rounds fired by the left-wing battery 'nearly missed' the Duke, while another 'took off two men exactly before him'. It is even said that his hat sustained some damage.

Cumberland's artillery opened fire two minutes later. He began to bring his front line forward to where the firm ground ended roughly 300 yards from the Jacobite lines. It halted where the tumble-down Leanach dyke ended about 100 yards west of the Well of the Dead. The infantry and artillery were thus dressed in line, with two cannon posted in the intervals between regiments.

Replying in kind, Major Belford ordered two of the cannon to be aimed at the knot of horsemen behind the Prince's standard, and several balls fell among the horses' legs. It was currently reported that Charles's face was spattered with mud, and that a servant, who was standing behind him with a led-horse, was killed. This later grew into the legend that Charles's horse was 'shot under him in the engagement, and that his groom was killed while he was mounting another'. In fact, the Prince *may* have been mounting a less conspicuous horse than Mr. Dunbar's grey gelding, but his luckless groom, Thomas Caw, was decapitated by a cannon ball some thirty yards off. The horse that he was leading is variously reported as having been hit in the haunch or in the shoulder, which in turn gave rise to a rumour that Charles was wounded in the thigh.

Some gentlemen from Inverness, who had posted themselves on a small hill not far from the Prince and his staff, 'were dislodged by cannon balls falling about them', and having lost their taste for battles, retired precipitately. The members of the royal *entourage* were equally shaken. Among them was Captain Daniel, the only English Jacobite officer known to have been present at Culloden, who carried the standard of the Prince's Life Guards. It had been captured from Gardiner's late regiment at Falkirk, and bore the singularly inappropriate motto of 'Britons, strike home!'. Describing this opening phase of the battle, Daniel wrote:

> 'The battle being now begun, the whole fury of the enemy's Artillery seemed to be directed against us in the rear; as if they had noticed where the Prince was. By the first cannon shot, his servant scarcely thirty yards behind him, was killed; which made some about the Prince, desire, that he would be pleased to retire a little off; but this he refused to do, till seeing the imminent danger from the number of balls that fell about him, he was by the earnest entreaties of his friends forced to retire a little off, attended only by Lord Balmerino's corps. Frequent looks and turns the Prince made, to see how his men behaved; but alas! our hopes were very slender. . . .'

After accompanying the Prince part of the way, Daniel was ordered to return to his former position, 'lest the sight of my standard going off, might induce others to follow'. He went back to find the spot 'covered with the dead bodies of many of the Hussars', who unfortunately for themselves had been moved from the left flank to the centre. They were later ordered by the Prince to return to the left, and the shelter of the hollow beside the south wall of the Culloden enclosures. Charles himself had ridden off to the right, passing to the rear of Avuchie's regiment and the cavalry forming the back-lying right wing of his second line. He spoke encouragingly to many of the men before posting himself slightly to the north-east of Culchunaig farm steadings.

Cumberland's cannonade was to exert a decisive effect on the course of the battle. For the first time during the campaign the Highlanders were exposed to the rapid and accurate fire of trained artillerymen, against which their own was feeble and ineffective. According to Dugald Graham, the rhyming historian, the Jacobite gunners were handicapped by the fact that they were shooting downhill:

> . . . *Twelve piece of cannon, but highly mounted;*
> *By which the gunners were affronted:*
> *For should they level ere so low,*
> *Shot, down a hill is loth to go;*

And though they ply'd them ne'er so warm
In such a posture could not harm.

While this may have been a contributory cause, the chief reason for the failure of the Prince's artillery was that it was 'ill-served and ill-pointed'. This is borne out by the fact that the left-wing battery was entirely without regular gunners, and was manned by scratch gun-crews, who were told to do the best they could. They succeeded in discharging only two of the pieces, and the battery's fire 'discontinued almost as soon as it began', for the amateur gunners fled when Belford's cannon 'began to play very briskly upon them'. The centre battery was little more effective, for the Jacobite artillerymen killed only five or six of the enemy, who were able to fire 20 shots to their one. Another, and less obvious reason for the ineffectiveness of the Jacobite artillery may have been the varied calibres of the guns, which must have complicated their ammunition supply.

Cumberland had at first assumed that his right wing 'was entirely secured', but his last advance had brought it beyond the protecting morass, and open country lay to the north of his first and second lines. He therefore ordered Pulteney's and Battereau's regiments from the reserve to take post on the right of the Royal and Howard's respectively, in the first and second lines. This left only Blakeney's, much under strength, in reserve. Although the Duke's lines 'outwinged the Prince's both to the right and to the left without the cavalry', he also took the precaution of posting Kingston's 200 horse on the gently rising ground to the right of Pulteney's men. They were presently joined by Cobham's 60 troopers, who on returning from patrol, took station on their flank. O'Sullivan had earlier noticed this party 'upon a hight at a great distance, but in a ligne with the right of the enemy', and Cumberland's officers had been doubtful whether it would return in time for the action.

The arrival of Cobham's men had far-reaching consequences. So, too, had Cumberland's decision to withdraw Wolfe's regiment from the extreme left of his second line and re-post it—*en potence*—at right angles to Barrel's, the left-hand regiment of the front line. Although now drawn up close to the north-east angle of the crumbling Leanach dyke, there had been some chance of Barrel's being outflanked, but Wolfe's men, posted on rising ground behind the dyke, were now in a position to open a deadly fire on the Highland right, should it make such an attempt. The cavalry on the left were equally

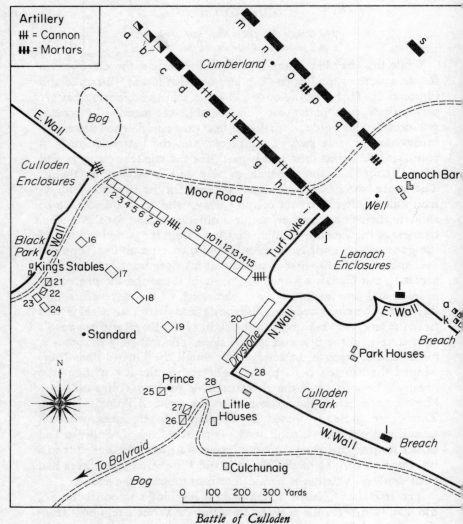

Artillery
‖‖‖ = Cannon
‖‖‖ = Mortars

Cumberland •

E. Wall

Bog

Culloden
Enclosures

Moor Road

Leanoch Bar

Well

Black
Park

King's Stables

Turf Dyke

Leanach
Enclosures

Standard

Drystone

N. Wall

E. Wall

Breach

Park Houses

Prince

Little
Houses

Culloden
Park

To Balvraid

Bog

W. Wall

Breach

Culchunaig

0   100   200   300 Yards

Battle of Culloden

Jacobite Army		Royal Army	
1 Glengarry	16 Irish Piquets	a Cobham's Dragoons	p Bligh
2 Keppoch	17 Royal Scots	b Kingston's Light Horse	q Sempill
3 Clanranald	18 Foot Guards	c Pulteney	r Ligonier
4 Duke of Perth	19 Ld. L. Gordon	d Royal Scots	s Blakeney
5 Glenbucket	20 Ld. Ogilvy	e Cholmondeley	
6 John Roy Stewart	21 Hussars	f Price	
7 Farquharson	22 Perthshire Horse	g Royal Scots Fusiliers	
8 McLean and McLachlan	23 Stonywood	h Munro	
9 Mackintosh	24 Bannerman	i Barrel	
10 Fraser	25 Balmerino's Life Guards	j Wolfe	
11 Appin	26 Ld. Elcho's Life Guards	k Ld. M. Kerr's Dragoons	
12 Cameron	27 FitzJames Horse	l Campbells	
13 1st Batt. ⎫ Atholl	28 Avuchie	m Battereau	
14 3rd Batt. ⎬ Brigade		n Howard	
15 2nd Batt. ⎭		o Fleming	

The Duke of Cumberland's position is marked by the small solid square between and in advance of Howard's regiment and
Fleming's (*n* and *o*). The small solid squares between and in advance of Fleming's regiment and Bligh's (*o* and *p*), and to the
left of Ligonier's (*r*), represent the cohorn mortars.

prepared. The remainder of Cobham's regiment, consisting of 240 men, and Kerr's three squadrons of 300 had taken post slightly to the left of Leanach barn. There they awaited orders to advance through the breaches in the park walls and fall upon the Prince's rear, as soon as his front line was engaged.

In contrast to Falkirk, the royal army had the advantage of the weather. Ray afterwards wrote: '. . . some Time was spent in striving who would gain the Flank; in which Interval a heavy Shower of Rain came on, which was very discouraging, remembering the Falkirk Affair; but now we had the Wind which was of some Comfort'. Actually this 'smart shower' had begun on Cumberland's first drawing up in face of the enemy. Other soldier writers, however, confirm Ray's statement that 'the weather grew fair' before the action began, one, Edward Lunn, going so far as to say that it had 'turned a fine day'. It is therefore clear that although the Highlanders' movements were impeded by wind and smoke, they were unaffected by hail, rain, or snow, as is generally supposed. On the other hand, the heavy shower must have been more detrimental to the Highlanders, with their old-fashioned muskets and powder-horns, than to the regular troops using cartridges, which were both quicker to fire and easier to keep dry.

The royal army was now drawn up in its final order of battle. From left to right Cumberland's front line consisted of the following seven regiments—Barrel's, Munro's, Campbells (Royal Scots Fusiliers), Price's, Cholmondeley's, the Royal, and Pulteney's—with Wolfe's *en potence* behind the Leanach dyke. Including Wolfe's, the front line totalled some 3,700 men.

In the same order, the second line, commanded by Major-General John Huske, consisted of Ligonier's, Sempill's, Bligh's, Fleming's, Howard's, and Battereau's regiments; while forming the reserve under Brigadier John Mordaunt, was Blakeney's.

Of the cavalry, 60 of Cobham's dragoons and Kingston's Light Horse were stationed on the right of the front line, the rest of Cobham's regiment and Kerr's three squadrons of dragoons being posted on the left of the front line, in the Leanach enclosure, slightly in front of the barn.

As a younger son, the Duke had small regard for his personal safety, and it has been said—perhaps unjustly—that in battle his one idea was to lead his men into the hottest part of the field and keep them there as long as possible. He was, however, a firm believer in the importance of leadership, and seeing in the MacDonalds' movement towards the enclosure wall an attempt to outflank his right, he had stationed himself in front of Howard's regiment, near the right of his second line. Weighing nearly 18 stone, and mounted on a powerful grey, the Duke must have been a conspicuous figure as he awaited the Highlanders' attack, which he expected them to launch from their left.

To hasten it, he ordered Major Belford to continue the cannonade, for, as Colonel Yorke wrote: 'When our cannon had fired about two rounds I could plainly perceive that the rebels fluctuated extremely and could not remain long in the position they were in without running away or coming down upon us.'

Although O'Sullivan had earlier admitted to Lord George that there was no choice other than these alternatives, he had apparently failed to impress this on his royal master. Charles's post at Culchunaig was ill-chosen for a commander-in-chief. The fact that Sir John MacDonald, who was with the Prince, saw only one man killed and thought the cannonade did little damage, proves fairly conclusively that, owing to the lie of the land, Charles can have had little idea of the havoc being wrought among his front-line troops. As a result of his inability to see what was happening, he thus gave Cumberland an unlooked-for opportunity of inflicting irreparable damage on the Highland army at small expense to his own.

Months of experience to the contrary had failed to shatter the Prince's belief that all would in the end be well, and he still did not doubt that 'the Duke would begin the attack as he had the wind and weather at his back'. But Cumberland, 'finding his cannon rapidly thinning the Jacobite ranks, without experiencing any loss in return', had no desire to attack. Although, according to Kirkconnel, many of their balls 'went over the Highland lines', Belford's five front-line batteries were doing great execution. They may have been assisted by two coehorn mortars, which in one plan of the battle are shown as firing over the royal front line from a position in rear of Cholmondeley's regiment and the Royal.

The duration of Cumberland's cannonade is variously estimated at from 25 to 30 minutes, and it has usually been assumed that for this length of time the Highland front line stood dumbly exposed to his devastating fire, awaiting the Prince's order to charge. Against this view, two contemporary writers state that only 15 or 20 minutes elapsed between the beginning of the cannonade and the start of the charge, and Campbell of Airds, who was guarding the baggage, has left it on record that what he calls 'the cannonade' lasted only nine minutes! Unfortunately he failed to make it clear what he meant by the word 'cannonade'. He certainly cannot have meant the whole period during which Cumberland's artillery was firing—there is too much evidence to show that this was for far longer than nine minutes—and it is more likely that he is referring to the time that elapsed from its opening fire to the charge of the Highland front line.

As the smoke from the royal artillery became more dense, it increasingly obscured the view of the Jacobite gunners. Under the personal direction of Lord George the guns on the right wing still managed to keep up a fire, but Belford's men had made 'a strange slaughter-house' of one of the other batteries—evidently that in the centre. In a gallant attempt to retrieve the situation, a French engineer, who had been late in arriving, brought up one of the two guns which earlier had had to be left behind. His helpers succeeded in hauling it to the south-east corner of the enclosure wall, although in this position its field of fire must have been severely limited.

It was at about this time that Major Belford ordered his gunners to load with grape-shot, which 'swept the field as with a hail storm', and the Highlanders, only partially inured to artillery, 'were greatly surprised and disordered' by it. The longer the cannonade continued the more unsettled they became. 'The regiments in the front rank ... were turned so impatient that they were like to break their ranks', wrote Lord George Murray, whose right-wing men, drawn up six deep, must have suffered most. A Lowland gentleman, serving in the front line, spoke for many years afterwards of the expressions of rage on the faces of the men beside him, and the Prince's only remaining hope of success would have been to have unleashed them while their blood was high and their ranks unthinned. Instead, great gaps were torn in the clan regiments, which had become so tightly packed by returning men that there were now no intervals between them, making it little wonder that Cumberland's map-makers found it impossible to identify them all. To escape the enemy's fire some threw themselves on the ground, 'some called out to advance, and a few broke their ranks and fled'. Among the last was an inn-keeper from Aviemore, who had been pressed into the army. He is said to have barely paused before regaining his inn, where later he was found in readiness to receive 'the aristocracy' of the defeated Jacobite army.

The Mackintoshes in the centre were particularly restive, and 'a message was sent along the line to Lochiel desiring he would represent to Lord George the necessity of attacking immediately'. To this Lochiel added the information that 'he could not hold his own men much longer', and realising that matters had reached a crisis, Lord George sent Ker of Graden to the Prince 'to know if he should begin the attack, which the Prince accordingly ordered. As the right wing was farther advanced than the left, Colonel Ker went to the left, and ordered the Duke of Perth, who commanded there, to begin the attack, and rode along the line till he came to the right, where Lord George Murray was, who attacked at the head of the Atholl men.'

Graden's account, although accurate as regards his own movements, suggests that he alone was entrusted with the Prince's order to begin the attack, and that it was received by Lord George after considerable delay. Both inferences, however, are misleading. For although there *was* some delay in the Prince's order reaching Murray, it was unconnected with Graden's round-about route, and was due to the fact that while on his way with it to Lord George, young MacLachlan of Inchconnel was decapitated by a cannon-ball.

To make certain that his instructions reached the front line, the Prince then sent Brigadier Stapleton to the right and Sir John MacDonald to the left, where Sir John found matters in an extremely unsatisfactory condition. On receiving the Prince's order from Graden, the Duke of Perth had immediately called on the Mac-Donalds to attack, but they had refused to obey him. He was soon afterwards joined by Lord John Drummond, who commanded the centre, but neither of the brothers could make any impression on the sullen clansmen. Seizing Clanranald's colour, the Duke exclaimed that if they beqaved with their accustomed valour he would change his name from Drummond to MacDonald, but his appeal was disregarded. The utmost they could be prevailed upon to do was to move forward until they were on a level with the other front-line regiments.

On the opposite wing the situation was very different. There, according to Kirkconnel, the Brigadier had no sooner delivered the Prince's order than it was obeyed, but by this time any such order was superfluous. For galled beyond endurance by Cumberland's artillery, and heedless of consequences, the Highland centre had surged forward from the line, to be followed almost immediately by the whole of the right wing. The attack had begun.

Leading the charge were the regiments of the Clan Chattan, which, in the absence of Lord John Drummond, were under the command of Colonel MacGillivray of Dunmaglas. Before the action strict orders had been given to the men to hold their fire 'until they could do certain execution', and that 'they must on no account fling away their muskets', but in the heat and excitement of the advance these instructions were forgotten. 'Their eagerness to come up with the enemy that had so much advantage of them at a distance, made them run on with the utmost violence, but in such confusion, that they could make no use of their firearms', and many 'threw them down without exploding them'.

Numerous accounts have been written of this heroic charge, led by the yellow-haired Dunmaglas, his standard bearer by his side. Few, however, stress the havoc caused by its sudden swing to the right, which prevented hundreds of the Prince's best men in the right-wing regiments from ever coming to grips with the enemy. The fatal swerve may have been caused by the fire of Cholmondeley's and Price's regiments, against which the attack of the Highland centre should have been directed, or by the boggy ground lying in the hollow between the two armies. The second of these reasons is the more probable, for the direction of the charge corresponds exactly with that of the old moor road, which presumably ran over firm ground.

Edward Lunn, who may have been one of Price's men, wrote home a graphic description of the Highlanders' attack:

> 'Their spirited advance lasted but a short time with any kind of warmth, and they shifted away to our left. They came up very boldly and fast all in a cloud together, sword in hand. They fired their pieces and flung them away; but we gave them so warm a reception that we kept a continued close fire upon them with our small arms; besides two or three of our cannon gave them a close fire with grape-shot, which galled them very much. . . . They thought it was such a bad day that our firelocks would not fire, but scarce one in our regiment missed firing, but kept them dry with our coat laps.'

The sudden alteration in the direction of the charge caused heavy casualties among the Highlanders, who were shot down like driven deer by the troops posted in the centre of Cumberland's front line. The fire of Campbell's Royal Scots Fusiliers was exceptionally steady, and although wounded, the brave young Dunmaglas refused to turn back. His standard bearer was shot dead, but Donald Mackintosh of Flemington seized the yellow banner of the clan and bore it onwards.

To Cumberland's men the fact that the wind was behind them was a tremendous advantage, for as one of them wrote, they could 'see the enemy clearly and neither have their nostrils filled with sulphur, nor their faces burnt with wadding'. Conversely, the smoke almost blinded the Highlanders, and it is doubtful if those of the Clan Chattan knew in which direction they were heading. One, indeed, later asserted that the first he saw of the enemy were the legs of their front-line men, as his clan closed in to attack.

At the beginning of the charge of the Jacobite centre, Lord George Murray had been talking to Lochiel, but within two minutes at most he had set the right wing in motion. Crowded against the park wall, and later the Leanach dyke, the tightly-packed regiments soon became inextricably mixed, and with those of the centre charged down upon the royal army's left wing 'in a Sort of a mob, without any order or distinction of Corps . . .'. Like those of the centre, many of the men of the right-wing regiments threw away their muskets without discharging them, for as Kirkconnel remarks, the congestion was so great 'that they could make no use of their fire-arms'. It became still worse on their reaching the projecting Leanach dyke, behind which Wolfe's regiment was posted, and partially protected, Wolfe's now opened a deadly flank fire on the crowded mass of men, herded together like a flock of sheep. Lord Nairne's men on the extreme right suffered most, Stewart of Killiechassie losing no fewer than 30 of the 33 men in his company. Nairne's brother, Robert Mercer of Aldie, was shot through the head, and neither his body, nor that of his son, Thomas—a cornet, though little more than a child—was ever found.

The full force of the charge fell upon Barrel's regiment and the left half of Munro's—a regiment that had fled at Falkirk, but whose officers and men were now determined to regain their lost laurels. With bayonets fixed, and drawn up in three ranks, the two regiments waited until the enemy was within 30 yards, when the centre and rear ranks fired. At such close quarters and with such a target it was next to impossible to miss—'like Wildcats their Men came down in Swarms upon our Left Wing', wrote a volunteer in Cumberland's army, '... they began to cut and Hack in their natural way without ceremony. ... When just near us and a fine mark, the King's men discharged a complete running Fire that Dropt them down as they came on.'

Yet despite their losses, the Highlanders' onslaught was unchecked, and those with muskets returned the redcoats' fire, notably the Camerons and the Athollmen. But as Lord George records:

'Their custome has always been when they do atact, to run upon the Enemy with the utmost speed so as only to receive one fire or at most two before they mixt. In the present case they were quite in disorder & received several fires before they could come up with the Enemy who stood upon their first ground, and the Highlanders lost the benefect [benefit] of their own fire, for only a few who run in quikest actually fird upon the Enemy. By far the grater Number, who followd as fast as they were able, could not fire as some of their own men were betwixt them and the Enemy. This was a vast loss for the ffire of Highlanders is more bloody then that of any regular troups whatever.'*

No two regiments could have been expected to withstand the impact of the eight clan regiments, numbering some 1,500 men, and Barrel's virtually split in two—whether by sheer weight of numbers or in obedience to Cumberland's command to let the enemy mingle with them is not clear. The fact that Lord Robert Kerr, who is said to have spitted the first oncoming Highlander—a Cameron—on his spontoon, failed to notice that his men had fallen behind him lends colour to the latter supposition. Before he could disengage the weapon he was surrounded and cut down, 'his head being cleft from crown to collar-bone', by Major Gillies MacBean of the Mackintosh regiment. Lieutenant-Colonel Rich, Barrel's young commander, not only had his left hand lopped off at the wrist, but had his right arm nearly severed above the elbow, and received six wounds in the head. He was carried out of danger by John Duncan, an army chaplain, who owed his appointment to Rich's father, Lieutenant-General Sir Robert Rich. Ensign Brown was wounded while defending the regimental colour, which, although knocked to the ground, was not captured by the enemy. An anonymous pro-Government account

* From an unpublished letter at Blair Castle.

related that:

> 'The Highlanders fought like furies and Barrel's behaved like so many heroes. It was dreadful to see the enemies' swords circling in the air as they were raised from the strokes: And no less to see the officers of the army, some cutting with their swords, others pushing with their spontoons, the sergeants running their halberts into the throats of the opponents, the men ramming their fixed bayonets up to the sockets.'

On being broken into, the men on the left wing of Barrel's were thrown outwards, thus making it more difficult for their attackers to find their way round the flank, while on the opposite wing the grenadier company was forced back into the interval between Munro's and Bligh's regiment in rear. Meanwhile, the fury of the Highlanders' attack remained undiminished:

> 'Making a dreadful huzza, and even crying "Run, ye dogs!", they broke in between the grenadiers of Barrel and Monro; but these had given their fire according to the general direction, and then parried them with their screwed bayonets. The two cannons on that division were so well served, that when within two yards of them they received a full discharge of cartridge shot, which made a dreadful havoc; and those who crowded into the opening received a full fire from the centre of Bligh's regiment, which still increased the number of the slain. However, such as survived possessed themselves of the cannon, and attacked the regiments sword in hand; but to their astonishment they found an obstinate resistance. . . .'

A vivid, but exaggerated, description of the part played by Munro's is given by the officer commanding its grenadier platoon, which, stationed on the left of the regiment, was in the thick of this fighting:

> 'Our lads fought more like devils than men. In short we laid (to the best of my judgment) about 1600 dead on the spot, and finished the affair without the help of any other regiment. You may judge of the work; for I had 18 men killed and wounded in my platoon. I thank God I escaped free, but my coat had six balls through it. In the midst of the action, the officer that led on the Camerons, called to me to take quarter; which I refused, and bid the rebel scoundrel advance. He did, and fired at me; but providentially missed his mark. I then shot him dead, and took his pistol and durk, which are extremely neat. No one that attacked us, escaped alive; for we gave no quarter nor would accept of any.'

The writer's efforts to enhance his regiment's reputation are more praiseworthy than convincing. For apart from his preposterous figure of the number of Jacobite dead, Munro's was far from finishing the affair unaided.

Cumberland, constantly on the move, and seeing his left hard pressed, sent orders by Yorke to Major-General Huske to bring up Bligh's and Sempill's in support. Having advanced some 50 yards, in accordance with the Duke's orders, they awaited the onset of the Highlanders, Bligh's covering the interval between Barrel's and Munro's. But so many of Barrel's men had crowded into the gap that not a great number of Highlanders can have fought their way through to engage Bligh's regiment, which suffered only light casualties.

Sempill's bore the brunt of the Jacobite attack. Noted for the accuracy of their fire, and having waited until their assailants had come very near, the men of the 25th 'gave a terrible fire that brought a great many of them to the ground, and made most of them that did not fall turn back'. Only the left half of the regiment could fire for fear of hitting Barrel's men—more of whom are said to have been killed by the fire of their friends than by the broadswords of their foes. With unconquerable courage the Highlanders struggled on through smoke that lay so low upon the field that they felt rather than saw their enemies. They were shot and mown down in heaps 'three or four deep . . . as they surmounted the dead bodies of their comrades'.

Huske could be heard shouting fiercely to his men: 'Give them the bayonet.' He was so well obeyed 'that hundreds perished on their points. . . . At the same instant the rebels, who came round the left of Barrel's, and in the pell-mell broke through the lines, met their fate from the fire of Wolfe's and Ligonier's on the left of the second line.'

Outnumbered as they were, Barrel's and Munro's men could not have put the new drill into practice, but those in the second line evidently did so, for one officer states that the directions 'made an essential difference, staggered the enemy who was not prepared to alter their way of fighting, and destroyed them in a manner rather to be conceived than told'. Some Highlanders, 'in their fury and despair, threw stones for at least a minute or two, before their total rout began'.

The situation had become catastrophic for the Prince's defeated followers, and it is graphically described in two seldom quoted contemporary accounts:

> '... an opening being made for a Party of them, who forced through our front Line, they were now between two Lines, and our Front completing again, they were severely handled both Ways: for those who escaped the fire of Bligh's and Sempill's Regiments met a worse Destruction from the Bayonets of our first Line, there being scarce one Soldier in Barrel's Regiment who did not each kill several Men, and they of Munro's which engaged did the same, besides what the Officers killed with their Spontoons.'

> 'Barrel's gallant regiment opened and received them between two fires: Lord Semple's Battalion, next in ye line, wheeled and enclosed them: a scene of carnage ensued: for they discharged with the muzzles of their guns at the rebels breasts, and stabbed em in the back with their Bayonets till they cut them off to a man. Some old military men said they never saw Corpses lye so thick, nor a field so strew with Officers, as that was after the Battle.'

Few of the 500 men thought to have penetrated Cumberland's lines won their way back to safety. Spent, and many of them wounded, with broken swords or without targes, they were now assailed from flank and rear by Barrel's men, who 'fairly beat them' with their weapons, and who are said to have accounted for almost their own number. There was scarcely an unwounded man who had not despatched one or two of the enemy, and whose bayonet was not bent and bloody.

Jacobite casualties were high among officers, and gentlemen of the clans serving in the front ranks as volunteers. Some of the rear ranks, comprised of boys and old or unwilling men, never came up with the enemy. 'Their commanders kept continually riding through their Lines forcing the Highlanders upon us', wrote a Whig volunteer. Lochiel, emerging from the *mêlée* to urge forward a party of his men, was hit in both ankles by grape-shot within pistol range of Barrel's regiment. Unable to walk, he was carried by two of his clansmen to a hut, which not long afterwards was surrounded by the enemy, but fortunately the troops were called off as they were about to enter it. His brother Archibald was also wounded, receiving a musket-shot which ran along the underside of his arm.

Leaderless and disheartened, the Camerons gave up their struggle against impossible odds. Other regiments did so too. Those who had fought their way back through Barrel's men now found themselves exposed not only to the fire of Wolfe's, but to the shells of a second-line mortar, and the grape-shot of two guns swiftly run forward from between Munro's and the Fusiliers to sweep the hillside up which the Highlanders must retreat.

Meanwhile, on the Jacobite left wing events had taken a very different turn. There, the only troops to have taken part in the charge was one company of Farquharsons. The clan was one of the few which had suffered severely for the part it had played in the '15, and in consequence many of the men had to be 'pressed'. Under such circumstances they showed 'a general disinclination to attack, which became more noticeable towards the left', where it was shared by Glenbucket's and John Roy Stewart's regiments, neither of which possessed swords.

The MacDonalds were equally unresponsive. Earlier, as already related, they had reluctantly moved up to the south-east corner of the enclosure wall, in which position they are depicted by Thomas Sandby, Cumberland's 'official artist', although to some of the Duke's officers they appeared to be slightly farther forward. Here they remained until shortly after the charge began, when on the orders of Lord John Drummond and O'Sullivan—so the latter claims—they again advanced, this time looking as if they intended to engage. They 'came running forward in their furious way on our right', wrote a royal army officer. 'They came down three several times within a hundred yards of our men, firing their pistols and brandishing their swords; but our brave soldiers appeared as if they took little notice of their bravado!'

Evidence to the same effect is given by Henderson, the Whig historian, and by Dugald Graham:

> 'The Duke's right stood and saw the fun,
> Some reg'ments never fir'd a gun;
> They only twice or thrice presented,
> But seeing them run it was prevented:
> For the order was, that fire they don't
> Till within few paces of their front.
> So when they see'd them so present,
> Back they fled with one consent,

Brandisht their swords and pistols fir'd,
Some threw their durks and then retir'd.

Following a military maxim of the period, which stressed the importance of getting the enemy to fire first, Lord John Drummond 'did all in his power to decoy the Royalists to give their fire at a distance that his wing might come in sword in hand . . . he even walked between the lines with his pike in his hand', but the Royal and Pulteney's on the Duke's right, posted on slightly elevated ground, refused to be tempted. But even had Lord John's coat-trailing tactics succeeded, it is more than doubtful whether the left wing could have been induced to attack. According to one Jacobite account, some of the MacDonalds had already been knee-deep in water, and between them and the enemy was swampy ground across which they would have had to charge. Moreover, they were being decimated by the fire of the battery opposite to them, and their feelings of insecurity were increased on seeing the motions of the Duke's cavalry, 'which began to move forward with the evident intention of outflanking them, which the infantry regiment [Pulteney's] on the extreme right was also in a position to do'.

The three MacDonald regiments were, in fact, 'in the air'. To their right rear the four other regiments comprising the Jacobite left wing—Perth's, Glenbucket's, Roy Stewart's, and the Farquharsons—were by now in flight, leaving a gaping void extending for hundreds of yards towards the opposite wing. Facing them were the menacing lines of Cumberland's disengaged front-line troops stretching far into the distance until they vanished in a low-hanging pall of smoke. Out of it there suddenly appeared running figures, and as the cloud thinned there could no longer be any doubt about the issue of the battle. The attack had failed, and the Jacobite right and centre were in full flight.

Outflanked and outnumbered, the MacDonalds were not slow in following their example.

'Lord John Drummond did all he could to stop the Flight . . . They threw down their firelocks, and began to give way; on which the right wing [Cumberland's] advancing some paces gave their fire in so close and full a manner that the ground was soon covered with the bodies of the dead and wounded, and the cannon being again loaded these fired into the midst of the fugitives and made a frightful carnage.'

The Duke of Perth, on seeing the failure of the attack, galloped over to the right in a vain but gallant attempt to stop the rout. Braving the enemy's artillery, he received a slight wound in the shoulder, only to die less than a month later on his way to France, worn out by the fatigues of the campaign.

Although the three MacDonald regiments 'drew off in an entire flight', some of their officers and men refused to retreat. The gentlemen of the clan had announced their determination to fight whether their followers did so or not, and they now kept their word. Exclaiming, 'O my God, has it come to this, that the children of my tribe have forsaken me!' Keppoch charged sword in hand towards the enemy lines, and his brother Donald, outstripping his own company in his eagerness to be the first to engage the enemy, was among the first to be shot down. Keppoch also fell, with a ball through his arm, and Donald Roy MacDonald, one of Clanranald's officers, entreated him not to throw his life away, but to retreat with his clan. So also did Mackenzie of Torridon, for the action was over and Cumberland's horse were scattering all over the field. Bidding Donald Roy take care of himself, Keppoch struggled on and received a second wound. He fell in front of Price's regiment. James Mac-Donald of Kilchonat endeavoured to help him off the field when yet another bullet hit the chief in the back. Kilchonat then ran on alone crying that Keppoch was dead, and thus demoralising his clansmen.

Clanranald was severely wounded in the head as he charged with his gentlemen and vassals. He managed to make his way to Inverness where his grandmother hid him in her house until he recovered sufficiently to return to his own country. Lochgarry was fortunate enough to be unwounded, but many of the Clan Donald officers lost their lives in that gallant charge, among them brave MacDonald of Scotus, who fell surrounded by 20 of his men.

The MacDonalds' foreboding about the intention of the enemy cavalry was fully justified. On seeing them retreat Cobham's 60 troopers at once moved forward, and encouraged by their example, Kingston's Horse were soon 'briskly falling in' with the fugitives. 'Keep close together, men', Torridon advised the Keppoch Mac-Donalds near him. 'If we stand shoulder to shoulder these men will be more frightened of us than we of them, but remember if you scatter they have four legs to each of your two, and singly you have small chance against them.' The men took his advice and were led from the field in fair order by Keppoch's natural son, nineteen-year-old Angus Ban.

After wheeling to the right to avoid a treacherous morass, Kingston's Light Horse swung smartly to the left and attacked the Royal Scots in the centre of the Jacobite second line, while Cobham's fell upon them from the rear. The Royal Scots, whose Lieutenant-Colonel, Lord Lewis Drummond, was badly wounded in the leg, were saved from complete encirclement by the Irish picquets, who had also come down from their post on the left of the second line, and whose close and steady fire covered the MacDonalds' retreat. The check was, however, only temporary, for with no other second-line troops left to sustain them, what remained of the Jacobite front-line regiments soon disintegrated. Game to the last, the Irish picquets took cover behind the boundary wall of what was known as the Black Park—one of the Culloden enclosures—and from this position they fired on the flank of the cavalry until it was out of range. Then, seeing the infantry about to advance, they retreated towards Inverness, carrying with them their wounded commanding officer, Brigadier Stapleton, who died of his injuries a few days later. Their gallant rearguard action cost them nearly a hundred lives— more than half their numbers on the field.

An equally gallant attempt to delay the pursuit was made by the gunners manning the single cannon sited at the south-east corner of the enclosure wall. Mounted on a large flat stone, its point-blank fire was so effective that one plan of the battle shows that no fewer than four of the 3-pounders and three coehorn mortars were run forward to silence it.

Two of Kingston's troopers were killed, but several were brought down both here and near the smithy on the road running beside the enclosure wall. The officers of the depleted Jacobite left had pressed into service every local man they could, including the black-smith:

> 'The smith, . . . a stalwart fellow, but not at all desirous to fight . . . snatched up the shaft of a cart that was reared against the wall of his smithy, he took his post beside them. When, however, he saw the havoc made by the English cavalry among his countrymen, his blood was up . . . and he laid about him with his tremendous weapon, knocking down the troopers from their horses, [until] beset by overwhelming numbers . . . he took the road to Inverness.'

As might have been expected, the casualties among the officers who had been in the forefront of the Jacobite attack were extremely heavy. The only regimental commanders to escape unwounded were Lord George Murray, Lord Nairne, and Ardshiel. No fewer than 19 officers of the Atholl Brigade were killed, while of the Mackintosh regiment only three survived. Of the rank and file of the centre and right-wing regiments which took part in the charge Lord George estimated that a third 'did not come off'.

He himself, at the head of the Athollmen, had 'behaved . . . with great gallantry, lost his horse, his periwig, and bonnet . . . had several cuts with broadswords[?] in his coat, and was covered with blood and dirt'. During the charge his horse had reared and thinking that it had been hit, he took a foot from the stirrup and was thrown. In the close-fighting he had lost one sword and broken another, but in spite of the noise and excitement of battle, he managed to retain his customary presence of mind. Realising only too clearly how the day was going, he forced his way through the crowd and hurried back to the second line to bring up reinforcements to the assistance of his hard-pressed men. He found little choice when he arrived there, for apart from the Irish picquets, the only second-line units left on the field were Lord Lewis Gordon's remaining battalion and Lord John Drummond's Royal Scots, commanded by his cousin, Lord Lewis Drummond. Led by Lord George, the two regiments advanced in good order towards the enemy and 'gave and received several fires', but by this time—in Kirkconnel's words—'the day was irrevocably lost; nothing could stop the Highlanders after they had began to run'.

The broken Jacobite right wing, and the Camerons in particular, received an unexpected check during their retreat along the side of the Leanach dyke. The Campbells had fired on them from the partial protection afforded by the crumbling dyke as they had advanced to the attack, and now that the tide had turned, the Argyll men not only opened fire again, but swarmed out from the park sword in hand. In the short and sharp encounter which followed, the Campbells lost half a dozen men and two officers. One of them was Archibald Campbell of Ballimore, commanding one of Lord Loudon's companies, who was shot dead while getting through 'a slap' in the dyke; the other, Captain John Campbell of Auchnabar, belonging to the Argyll Militia, died of his wounds the following day. The

Camerons' casualties are unknown, and having shown their age-old enemies that they could still fight back, they continued their retreat.

Spurred on by this success, the Campbells advanced farther on to the moor, afterwards bragging that they had forced Lord John Drummond's Royal Scots to withdraw, but it is more probable that this regiment was intentionally moving towards the left to assist the Irish picquets in covering the MacDonalds' retreat. Nevertheless, although they cannot have followed up far, the Campbells had some grounds for claiming that they 'were the only foot who pursued, and that the regular foot did not advance a step after the action'.

Meanwhile the rest of the 140 Campbells on Cumberland's left wing had rendered equally valuable service. Having gained access to the upper Culloden park through the breaches made by the Argyll Militia in the eastern park wall, Hawley with Cobham's and Lord Mark Kerr's dragoons had ridden up the hill. After dividing the five squadrons into ten half-squadrons he and Bland proceeded to carry out the flanking movement that Lord George had expected.

The main body of the cavalry encountered no resistance as it advanced westwards across the park, but two half-squadrons of Kerr's and the Glenorchy and Nether Lorn companies of the Campbells, which had been dispatched towards the north-west corner of the park, met with some slight opposition from a party of Jacobite infantry 'that lay under a wall firing'. According to Enoch Bradshaw—an unpleasant fanatic, who claimed descent from the regicide—three of his fellow troopers were shot dead by these nameless heroes, who were 'killed to a man'. It is probable that they belonged to Gordon of Avuchie's regiment, posted a little distance outside the west wall, for Lord George emphatically states that the enemy approached the wall 'without receiving a shot from the regiment ordered to guard it'. In thus blaming Lord Ogilvy's regiment which he had left to guard the wall, Murray seems to have been unaware that young Ogilvy and his men had been withdrawn to form a reserve, with instructions not to fire unless ordered to do so. Why, and by whom, such idiotic orders were given has never been revealed.

In accordance with them, the Angus men were now drawn up in square some distance from the north-west corner of the park, and using the dyke as a breast-work, the Argyll Militia fired 'briskly upon them and did considerable execution (with no loss to themselves who were under cover) for though few were killed by reason of the distance yet many were wounded, especially in the legs and thighs'.

Meanwhile a party of Campbells had made a breach in the west wall, wide enough for the cavalry to pass through three abreast, and advancing through it in half-squadrons, the dragoons crossed the track leading from Culchunaig to the ford over the Nairn, and took up position 'about the houses of Culchunaig'.*

Why this encircling movement, only less decisive than Cumberland's artillery fire, was allowed to succeed can be ascribed to a variety of reasons. Lord George, before the action began, had been apprehensive that such a movement might be attempted, but owing to the small numbers of troops which had then arrived had considered himself unable to spare any to guard the parks. O'Sullivan, on his own showing, had been equally alive to the danger, but had later decided that it could be discounted. As for the Prince, he may well have accepted O'Sullivan's assurances at their face value, but the fact remains that had he been nearer the front line he would have been able to take the necessary action. For, as the Chevalier Johnstone remarks: 'It was evident our destruction became inevitable, if the English got possession of the inclosure', and in trying to fight the battle by remote control, Charles forfeited any slender chance he might have had of winning it.

Observing the position of the enemy cavalry, 'Lord George ordered the [Life] Guards and Fitzjames' horse quite to the right flank, and made them form opposite to the dragoons, upon the brink of a hollow way; the ascent was somewhat steep on both sides, so that neither could pass safely in presence of the other.' As he had shown on many occasions during the campaign, Lord George had an exceptionally good eye for country. Earlier in the day the Atholl Brigade had been posted immediately in front of this narrow sunken lane, and now making skilful use of it he was to be responsible for saving many hundreds of lives.

The Prince's once proud force of 400 well-mounted cavalrymen had latterly shrunk to a pitiful collection of 'incomplete troops', whose half-starved horses were hardly fit for service. Lord Pitsligo's

* The tenant had betaken himself across the river with a baby in his arms and a toddler in a sack on his back. His wife remained baking throughout the battle until a wounded Highlander ran into her kitchen and thrust the bleeding stump of his severed arm upon her red-hot girdle.

Horse, once 150 strong, had 'dwindled away to nothing'; Lord
Kilmarnock's squadron had been re-formed as a regiment of foot,
and of Lord Elcho's and Lord Balmerino's Life Guards, originally
totalling 150 men, only some 46 were present at Culloden. These
reductions had been partly offset by detachments of Fitz James's
Horse, which had arrived from France during the winter, but as
many of their chargers had been captured at sea, they were similarly
'ill-mounted'. In addition, large numbers of them had surrendered
on the march northwards, and they now amounted to no more than
70 men, commanded by Colonel Robert O'Shea.

Drawn up on the north side of the hollow in accordance with Lord
George's orders, the two squadrons under Elcho and O'Shea can
have had small hope of survival, for although Avuchie's regiment
was posted between them and the west wall it was fully occupied
in watching the Campbells. Opposing them were between 400 and
500 of Kerr's and Cobham's men well-mounted and well-armed, but
so firm and resolute was the Jacobites' demeanour that it was not
until ten minutes had elapsed that they dared to attack. Although
Elcho and his Major, Kirkconnel, left detailed and well-informed
accounts of the campaign, they seldom refer to their own exploits
and this incident is barely mentioned by either. Yet it was the
delaying action of their men and Fitz James's that allowed the right
wing of the Jacobite army to make its escape. Fitz James's Horse
suffered heavy losses during the action.

On moving to the left, probably with the intention of covering
the retreating MacDonalds, the Royal Scots found themselves almost
surrounded. After trying unsuccessfully to join his regiment, Lord
John met Captain Daniel, who had apparently handed his standard
to William Home, a fourteen-year-old cornet in Balmerino's troop,
who had borne it at Falkirk. Agreeing that all was over, the two men
went hastily up the hill towards the retreating right wing. 'The men
in general were taking themselves precipitately to flight; nor was
there any possibility of their being rallied', wrote Robert Strange.
'The greater numbers of the army were already out of danger. . . .
We got upon a rising ground, where we turned round and made a
general halt.'

The Highlanders' movements were closely watched by Cumberland's officers, who at first supposed that this pause might indicate
a renewal of the attack. But O'Shea's and Elcho's squadrons had at

last been forced to give way before the dragoons, and before they could be formed up in square, as Lord John intended, O'Sullivan suddenly galloped up from the rear. Excitedly addressing O'Shea, he ordered him to escort the Prince from the battlefield: 'Yu see all is going to pot. Yu can be of no great succor, so before a general deroute wch will soon be, Seize the Prince & take him off.' The Adjutant-General added the gratuitous advice that if O'Shea found that he was being followed by the enemy dragoons, he should 'stand firm' so as to allow the Prince time to escape. With his usual lack of balance O'Sullivan was panicking unnecessarily, for Charles was so far in rear that he was in no danger of being captured, yet O'Shea was left with no alternative but to obey, and

> Fitz James's horse, for all their pride,
> Unto the rear were fain to ride.

Descriptions of the Prince's behaviour in these last bitter moments of defeat show a wide variation—from rank cowardice to a heroic determination to die with his men, depending largely upon the writer's personal and political views.

That he endeavoured to rally some regiments is certain, and it is equally clear that they can only have been those on the left wing, which fled before the Highland attack was repulsed, namely, Stoneywood's, Bannerman's, the Farquharsons, Perth's, Glenbucket's, and John Roy Stewart's. His retreat from the field with the two last-named regiments also supports this belief. The fact that the dragoons were now at Culchunaig likewise proves conclusively that the Prince must have been at Balvraid when he attempted to intercept his retreating forces, and since this was a mile from the enemy front line, it is hardly surprising that there is no record of Cumberland's men having caught sight of him.

An interesting account of the Prince's movements at this time is given in a little-known history of the Rising compiled from information given by his Italian valet, Michele Vezzosi:

> He saw with astonishment these troops which he had looked upon as invincible, flying before the enemy in the utmost disorder and confusion. In vain did he strive to reanimate and persuade them to return to the charge; the mouths of murdering cannon spoke a louder and more persuasive language than all his promises and entreaties could do, though uttered in the most moving terms, such as these: 'Rally, in the name of God. Pray, gentlemen, return. Pray

stand with me, your Prince, but a moment—otherwise you ruin me, your country and yourselves; and God forgive you.'

In such-like terms as these he addressed every corps he saw retreating. But to no purpose; the consternation was too general to admit of remedy; neither did the greatest part of them understand what he said, and such as did cried out: 'O unhappy Prince! O, fatal day! In what destruction have we involved our country and our friends.'

While he was in this confusion and endeavouring to stop the torrent of his men's flight, his wig and bonnet blew off; the last it's said was taken up by one of his friends and presented to a gentle-woman of the Roman Catholick religion, who kept it as a sacred relic. . . . His wig he recovered as it was falling from the pommel of the saddle.

Although it is extremely unlikely that Vezzosi was an eye-witness, and despite its high-falutin' style, the passages describing the Prince's inability to make his followers understand what he said, and the blowing away of his bonnet and wig, would seem to lend authenticity to his account.

Charles's old tutor, Sir Thomas Sheridan, and others belonging to his inner circle besought him to think of his own safety now that all was lost, but 'he could scarcely believe he was struck with so severe an affliction'. He seems, indeed, to have been overcome by indecision, and seizing his bridle, Lochiel's uncle, Major Kennedy, forced him from the field.

Accompanied by Hay of Restalrig, Sir Thomas Sheridan, and a number of Scots officers, the Prince, escorted by O'Shea and his men, rode towards the ford of Faillie over the Nairn. On halting at the ford, where he was joined by Elcho and O'Sullivan, the Prince held a meeting to discuss what was to be done. According to Elcho, he was 'in a deplorable state' and obsessed by the idea that the Scots intended to betray him. On seeing more and more Scots officers arriving, 'he ordered them to go away to a village a mile's distance from where he was, and he would send his orders thither'. To Elcho 'he appeared to be concerned only about the lot of the Irish and not at all about that of the Scots', and he adds the almost incredible statement that the Prince 'neither Spoke to any of the Scots officers present, or inquired after any of the Absent,* (nor at any of the preceding battles he never had inquired after any of the wounded Officers)'.

* He did, in fact, inquire for Lord George Murray.

Having gone 'aside' with his little clique of favourites, Charles decided to push on towards the Fraser country. Meanwhile, he sent orders to the officers at the village to proceed to Ruthven, where they would receive further instructions, but they were barely a mile on their way before a second message arrived from him, ordering them to disperse.

To the sound of a Fraser's pipes, and with flying colours, the Jacobite right wing carried out its retreat 'with the greatest regularity'. That it succeeded in doing so was due mainly to Lord George Murray, and to Lord Ogilvy and his two battalions from Angus, commanded by himself and Sir James Kinloch. Ogilvy, aged 21, had held a commission in the French army, and was very popular with his men. His regiment had retreated northwards by way of its own country, and although nearly 100 men had failed to rejoin it, the two battalions were still some 550 strong and had sustained few casualties in the battle. The Angus men were the best equipped, and according to some accounts, the best disciplined in the Prince's army, and they now showed their quality. In square formation they faced about several times during the early stages of the withdrawal, and by keeping Hawley's cavalry in check, were able to prevent the rear of the right wing from being cut to pieces.

According to the Chevalier Johnstone, the royal cavalry seems to have treated the right wing with considerable respect. During the retreat to Faillie it was confronted by a party of dragoons 'which appeared as much embarrassed as the Highlanders; but the English commander very wisely opened a way for them in the centre, and allowed them to pass at the distance of a pistol shot without attempting to molest them or to take prisoners'. The only exception was one officer:

'who wishing to take a Highlander prisoner, advanced a few paces to seize him, but the Highlander brought him down with his sword, and killed him on the spot; and not satisfied with this, he stopt long enough to take possession of his watch, and then decamped with the booty. The English commander remained a quiet spectator of the scene, renewed his orders to his men not to quit their ranks, and could not help smiling and secretly wishing the Highlander might escape on account of his boldness, without appearing to lament the fate of the officer, who had disobeyed his orders.'

Although some doubt is cast on this story on account of the fact that no cavalry officer is shown among the royal army's casualties, it lends support to Kirkconnel's statement that Cumberland's mounted troops were disinclined to attack any Jacobite units that remained unbroken, but 'contented themselves with sabering such unfortunate people as fell in their way single and disarmed'.

Having received no orders from the Prince, and apparently knowing nothing of his instructions to the other officers to disperse, Lord George and the right, on reaching Faillie, took the road for Ruthven of Badenoch.

Unlike the orderly retreat of the Jacobite right wing, that of the left was little better than a rout. Although by now only the dead and wounded remained on the field, Cumberland's artillery fire continued, and this phase of the battle is described by Edward Lunn: 'A few royals [mortars] sent them a few bombs and cannon balls to their farewell, and immediately our horse that was on the right and left wings pursued them with sword and pistol and cut a great many of them down so that I never saw a small field so thick with dead.'

The cavalry from both wings had met in the centre of what had been the Prince's second line. Under Lieutenant-Colonel Lord Ancrum and Major-General Bland, Kingston's and part of Cobham's were ordered to carry on the pursuit as far as they could, while the rest under Hawley, undertook mopping-up operations on the field. In the course of them some of his cavalry dismounted and left their horses in the outbuildings of the house since known as 'The King's Stables'. The pursuing cavalry followed the MacDonalds, and the centre regiments which had taken the road to Inverness. Exhausted Highlanders, who had been roused from sleep in the neighbouring enclosures, swelled the crowd of fugitives, and the pursuit was hottest at the White Bog, near the Mackintosh ancestral burial-ground, where many of the clan were slain. Even non-combatants were not immune. Two old weavers were killed at Ballavraat, and a man and his little son were wantonly slain in a ploughed field through which the troopers passed, while one young woman was only saved by falling on her knees and praying to be spared. It was not until the King's Mill was reached—a mile short of the town— that the last fugitive was killed. Among the last to be struck down was the blacksmith from Culloden.

Many contemporary writers have left descriptions of the pursuit

—of fugitives hacked cruelly by the swords of their pursuers, or ridden down and 'their brains beaten out by the horses'—and Henderson, Cumberland's biographer, wrote:

'... they were pursued by Kingston's Light Horse, and mangled terribly, while the Soldiers, warm in their Resentment, stabbed some of the wounded. A Party meeting others at Culloden House brought them forth and shot them. ... The Troops were enraged at their Hardships and Fatigues during a Winter campaign; the habit of the enemy was strange, their Language was still stranger, and their mode of Fighting unusual; the Fields of Preston and Falkirk were still fresh in their Memories.'

Kingston's men were anxious to wipe out old scores. In the skirmish at Keith two of them had been killed and 24 wounded or captured, and for their zeal during the pursuit three troopers were specially commended by Cumberland. Significantly, all three were Nottingham butchers. Bland also received a 'mention' for his services. According to the Duke's official despatch he 'made a great slaughter, and gave quarter to none but about fifty French officers and soldiers he picked up in his pursuit'. Lord Ancrum was equally merciless, except to Lord Kilmarnock, who had mistaken a party of royal cavalry for one of Fitz James's Horse. Recognising the Earl, he saved him from being shot on the spot, and later broke the news of his capture as kindly as he could to Kilmarnock's son, Lord Boyd, who was serving in the royal army.

The commanders of the Hussars and the Perthshire Horse had remained on the field. Colonel Bagot was taken prisoner, but Lord Strathallan, 'resolving to die in the field rather than by the hand of the executioner', apparently charged towards the enemy. His horse fell under him, and he attacked Colonel Howard who ran him through the body. The Sacraments were administered to the dying man by James Maitland of Careston, a non-juror, acting as chaplain to the Mackintosh regiment. Only oatcake and whisky could be obtained for the purpose.

MacLean of Drimnin, most of whose followers had been killed, made a desperate attempt to return to the field in search of his missing sons. Two of Cobham's troopers intercepted him. He rushed upon them, shot one dead and wounded the other. Three of their comrades, hurrying to their assistance, cut the unfortunate colonel to pieces. Major Gillies MacBean, one of the Mackintosh regiment, wounded and weaponless, was overtaken by the dragoons at

Balvraid. Leaning with his back against a wall, he seized the 'tram' of a small cart, and is said to have defended himself with it until he was overpowered.

Having left the immediate pursuit to his cavalry, Cumberland slowly followed with the infantry and artillery. On seeing the MacDonalds falling back, the Campbells who formed the Duke's baggage-guard had rushed forward to the front line in hopes of speeding their hereditary enemies, but Cumberland was in no great hurry to follow up. Instead, he ordered the regiments to 'stand upon the ground where they had fought and dress their ranks', and only then was the advance continued, less Barrel's and Munro's regiments, which were left behind to lick their wounds.

'As the Dukes army after the deroute Continued to pursue in order of Battle', wrote Elcho, 'always firing their Cannon and platoons in Advancing, their was not so many people kill'd or taken as their would have been had they detach'd Corps to pursue, but Every body that fell into their hands gott no quarters, except a few they reserv'd for publick punishment. . . .' Among these last was his friend Lord Balmerino, who gave himself up the following day, against Elcho's advice. For the rest there was no mercy, and an eye-witness says that the moor 'was covered with blood, and our men, what with killing the enemy, dabbling their feet in the blood, and splashing it about one another, looked like so many butchers'.

Their Commander-in-Chief, who was to earn this very soubriquet, had no compunction in setting them an example. As he rode over the field of battle he noticed the wounded Fraser of Inverallochy staring at him and his staff, and when asked to whom he belonged, the twenty-year-old colonel replied, 'To the Prince.' On receiving this answer, the Duke ordered Major Wolfe to shoot the insolent scoundrel, to which the future conqueror of Quebec replied that although his commission was at the Duke's service, he refused to act as an executioner. His humanity, however, was unavailing, and the order was carried out by a soldier.

Of Cumberland one of his soldiers wrote, 'his presence was worth five thousand men', and wherever he rode he was greeted with tumultuous cheering. There were shouts of 'Now Billy, for Flanders!', for having defeated the rebels his men were eager to return to what they considered their real business—fighting the French. He had special words of thanks for his 'brave Campbells',

'Wolfe's boys' and Barrel's, Munro's and Sempill's. Many of the other regiments, as one contemporary pointed out, had had small share in the action, but their officers and men had 'desired nothing more than a general engagement, every one of them being in high spirits, and willing to exert themselves in their several stations'.

From the 'Field of Battle near Culloden Park' their Commander-in-Chief issued the following order:

> 'The Surgeons to take immediate Care of the wounded. The Army and Artillery to form Columns and march through Inverness to Camp. The QMrs and 6 men per company to go back for the tent poles, and bring them up with the Battn Horses. Lord Sempills Regt to March forward to Inverness and take charge of the Town and the Prisoners there. Cavalry to pursue the Enemy as fast as they can.'

Soon distracted camp-followers were scrambling about the field searching for their men among the dead and the wounded, who were now being lifted into the bat-wagons that had trundled on to the moor. But of the beggars on their way to pillage the slain, many had been cut down by the troopers, and others lay among the ashes of the burnt-out Leanach barn.

Cumberland is said to have eaten his deferred mid-day meal on the stone that bears his name. He expressed 'Sympathizing tenderness for the wounded', and directed that rum, brandy, biscuit and cheese, should be sent up for his men from the provision ships in the firth.

> 'Each having taken his Quota, they advanced huzzaing, throwing up not only their Hats, but some Bonnets into the Air, while the Transports discharged a round for Victory; and though exulting in the Jollity, yet when near Inverness they appeared somewhat concerned at the Case of the miserable People whose Carcasses lay strewn in the Way.'

> 'The Duke of Cumberland marching towards Inverness was met by a drummer with a message from Gen. Stapleton offering to surrender, and asking for quarter, the Duke made Sir Joseph Yorke alight from his horse and with his pencil write a note to Gen. Stapleton assuring him of fair quarter, and honourable treatment. The drummer went off with his answer. The Duke then sent forward Capt. Campbell of Sempill's Regiment with his company of grenadiers, who took possession of Inverness.'

This company was led by James Campbell, of Ardkinglass, and his men, and those that came after them presented a strange and alarming spectacle to Jacobite sympathisers in the town. Having stripped the dead and wounded on the battlefield, they had arrayed themselves in such an assortment of laced hats, coats, waistcoats, and bonnets adorned with feathers, that it was at first supposed almost every chief and person of distinction in the Prince's army had been killed.

> 'His Highness entered Inverness at the head of the dragoons, all bespattered with... dirt and sweat, and his sword in his hand. The bells were set aringing, and people gave the signal to huzza; but he moved his hand to give over, and calling for the keys of the prison ordered the doors to be set open and the prisoners to be brought forth. Liberty was the first fruit of his conquest, and as the confined men came down stairs he clapped them upon the shoulder, saying: "Brother soldiers, you are free," ordered an entertainment for them, and payment of all arrears. About four o'clock the whole army came in. They advanced huzzaing, and seemed to be prodigiously pleased; and what tended to heighten the satisfaction was that from the time of his entering Inverness prisoners were either brought to him in troops, or else submitted themselves.'

The released prisoners, to whom a guinea a-piece was given, in compensation for their confinement, were for the most part Argyll militiamen, captured during the raid on the Atholl outposts. On reaching Inverness they had been stripped of their clothing by an officious Jacobite officer, whose men were ill-equipped, but Lord George had wrathfully demanded its immediate return. Since then, thanks to the kindly supervision of his brother and Lord Kilmarnock, they had been well cared for.

The prison was no sooner emptied of the soldiers of King George than its gates reopened to admit those of King James, and the church and other buildings were later requisitioned to house them. The Royal Scots, in their blue coats faced with red, and what were left of the Irish picquets were drawn up in line, standing behind their surrendered arms, hemmed in by the cavalry and Sempill's grenadiers; and other prisoners were hourly being brought in. The Duke released all delinquents from his own army, and ordered his Secretary, Sir Everard Fawkener, to give 12 guineas from his own purse to every wounded soldier—a generous sum, for there were 259 of them. Sixteen guineas were presented to every man who had taken an enemy standard, and these were later borne by chimney-sweeps through the streets of Edinburgh to be burned with the Prince's Standard by the public hangman.

Cumberland slept in the dowager Lady Mackintosh's house—the best in the town—'pleased to take his lodging where young Charly had just before kept his Court'. His hostess was less delighted. 'I've had two king's bairns living under my roof in my time,' she afterwards said, 'and to tell you the truth, I wish I may never have another.'

Out on the grim moor, six miles away, lay the Duke's fallen adversaries, many of the wounded still lying naked among the dead. They were left untended by the army surgeons who, apparently, believed the lie that Cope's men had lain neglected for two days and nights on the field of Prestonpans, just as the officers and men of Cumberland's army credited the equally unsubstantiated story that no quarter was to be given by the Jacobites at Culloden. Lady Findlater and her husband, whose house at Cullen had been plundered by the Jacobites, had watched the battle from a distance; and as her ladyship followed Cumberland to Inverness, her coachman struck viciously with his whip at MacDonald of Belfinlay, who lay helpless on the moor.

But three brave, determined women, their hearts full of pity for the suffering, had set out from Inverness for the battlefield, which they reached about half-past three in the afternoon. They were a Mrs. Stoner and a Mrs. Leith, and the latter, a connection of Gordon of Glenbucket, was accompanied by her maid Eppy. They were allowed to minister to the wounded, although it is unlikely that they were given the use of the medical stores, brought up by Lord George's orders from Atholl, where Lord Lewis Gordon's men had carelessly left them. Fortunately, these early precursors of Florence Nightingale had brought what they could in their baskets, and to them not a few of the Prince's wounded followers owed their lives.

8

Epilogue

ALTHOUGH CULLODEN was fought little more than 200 years ago, certain legends have grown up around the battle which by repetition have acquired the hall-mark of authenticity.

Perhaps the most persistent is the belief that the battle was a latter-day Flodden, waged between English and Scots, but nothing could be further from the truth. For of Cumberland's 15 regular battalions, no fewer than three regiments (1st, 21st, and 25th Foot) were Scottish, and to these must be added the companies of Lord Loudon's regiment and those of the Argyll Militia. Following the same line of thought it is also frequently assumed that the atrocities perpetrated after the action were carried out at the instigation of English officers, whereas three of the worst offenders—Major Lockhart, Captain Scott, and the naval officer, Fergussone—were Lowland Scots.

There are, too, the exaggerated tales of valour, which were circulated by the Jacobites to mitigate the bitterness of their defeat. There is the assertion by one of the Mackintoshes, few of whom attacked Barrel's, that only two men of the regiment were left standing after it had been mauled by the Clan Chattan. Yet, of Barrel's 438 officers and men, the casualty lists disclose that not more than 17 were killed and 108 wounded. Again, although the total Government casualties are given as 50 killed, 259 wounded, and one missing, of whom only six of the dead were cavalrymen, writers still blandly recount how Gillies MacBean killed 13 dragoons single-handed. Moreover, if to his victims are added the 19 men alleged to have been slain by Big John MacGillivray and a deaf and dumb Fraser, only 18 fatal casualties remain to be accounted for by the rest of the Jacobite army.

There also exists the belief that, because none of the 222 French and 336 Scots prisoners at Inverness is listed as wounded, this provides evidence that the Jacobites found lying wounded on the field of battle were done to death. While many undoubtedly were, it was not then the custom to differentiate between wounded and unwounded prisoners, and proof that many of the prisoners at Inverness were wounded is contained in a number of reports concerning their callous treatment. It is certain, however, that there were fewer than would have been the case had the engagement been between regular troops. For knowing that as rebels they could expect little mercy from the royal army, the Highlanders carried off as many of their wounded as possible, and the bodies of some who had died in making their escape were found 20 miles from the battlefield.

Contrary to popular tradition the numbers of men who actually took part in the fighting were remarkably small, for although about 14,000 are estimated to have been present at the battle, probably fewer than 3,000 were actively engaged. Of Cumberland's army, two regiments in the first line, two in the second, and one in the reserve, and the main body of the Campbells, never discharged their muskets. Three of his front-line regiments fired upon the charging Highlanders from a distance, and Ligonier's in the second line repulsed only a few spent men. On the opposing side, no more than eight of Charles's 22 regiments either charged or came within musket-range of Cumberland's front line; while of the Jacobite second line, only five or six infantry and two cavalry units fired when covering the retreating front line. One Highland and three Lowland foot regiments and two cavalry formations actually left the field without firing a shot.

On the morning after the battle, the officers and men of the Jacobite right wing fell in with Cluny and 300 to 400 of his clan at Dalmagarry, near Loch Moy. Cluny had learned of the previous day's disaster from a party of FitzJames's Horse, and Lord George now ordered him 'to remain till the rear of the defeated army came up, which might take about two hours, and then to cover the rear'. On reaching Ruthven patrols were sent out to guard the approaches to Badenoch, and a messenger was sent to the Prince by Lord George, informing him that he had a great part of the army with him—some 1,500 men, it is estimated—but that except for Cluny and Ardshiel all the chiefs 'were a-missing'.

Charles had spent the early part of the night of the battle at Gorthlick, about 20 miles from Culloden, where for the first and last time he met old Lord Lovat. From there his aide-de-camp MacLeod, wrote to tell Cluny that, in spite of that morning's 'ruffle', it was intended 'to review to-morrow at Fort Augustus the Frasers, Camerons, Stewarts, Clanranalds, and Keppoch's people'. The messenger who brought this letter seems to have let fall the information that the Prince was now on his way to Glengarry, and when returning it to Cluny, Lord George wrote: 'Mr. McLeod's letter seems to be a state of politicks I do not comprehend.'

It is evident that until the arrival of this letter the officers at Ruthven knew nothing about the proposed rendezvous, the object of which appeared to them to be that of deceiving the Prince's enemies, and enabling him to escape. To add to their surprise and indignation they learned that Michael Sheridan, Sir Thomas's nephew, had been ordered to carry back to the Prince the money he had given Aeneas MacDonald at the Ford of Faillie to distribute among his needy followers. As Lord George Murray angrily exclaimed: 'It is a very hard case that the Prince carries away the money while so many gentlemen who have sacrificed their fortunes for him are starving. Damn it! If I had ten guineas in the world I'd with all my heart and soul share it with them.'

Even the rich and generous Perth had nothing to give them, for his equipage had fallen into enemy hands in the parks of Culloden, as had also the bags of meal brought there too late to feed the Prince's starving followers. Nor was the supply position at Ruthven any better, for although Lord George had entreated that stores of meal might be sent to Badenoch in case of a reverse, he found nothing there with which to feed his men. It is small wonder that he wrote a letter of angry recrimination to his royal leader, who had dealt so callously with his loyal adherents.

Whether the Prince received this letter is unknown, but the following day, and apparently without words of gratitude, there came his last brief royal command: 'Let every man seek his own safety the best way he can.' It was read out to his assembled followers by Lord George Murray and Lord John Drummond, and the Chevalier Johnstone has left a vivid picture of their sorrowful leave-taking:

'Our separation at Ruthven was truly affecting. We bade one

another an eternal adieu. No one could tell whether the scaffold would not be his fate. The Highlanders gave vent to their grief in wild howlings and lamentations; the tears flowed down their cheeks when they thought that their country was now at the discretion of the Duke of Cumberland, and on the point of being plundered; whilst they and their children would be reduced to slavery, and plunged, without resource into a state of remediless distress.'

That bitterness mingled with their grief is evident from some of the memoirs of the officers ruined in the Prince's service. Lord George's is thinly-veiled in the notes he jotted down soon after Culloden for a projected history of the campaign, but considerably softened when these took the form of 'Marches of the Highland Army'. He and other leaders had torn themselves reluctantly from their families to embark upon an enterprise, the success of which they doubted. Loyalty to their King, and a desire to re-establish Scotland's independence and sweep away corrupt Whig administration, had brought them into the field. By the chiefs, a rising was no longer looked upon as a heaven-sent opportunity for wreaking vengeance on hereditary foes, and seizing their lands and cattle. The thoughts of men like Keppoch and Lochiel were rather for bettering the condition of their people, and enforcing order in their territories, and they and others had a regard for the lives of their men unknown in the '15.

Lord George never saw the Prince again. After hiding for eight months in Glenartney, he escaped abroad and visited Holland and Rome. He chose Germany as his place of exile, but travelled extensively, and died in 1760 at Medemblik in Holland. Lord John Drummond died of fever at Bergen-op-Zoom the year after Culloden, while Lord Ogilvy, after hiding among the rocks by Loch Wharral in Glen Clova, sailed to Norway. From there he made his way to France, where he became a general in the French army, eventually regaining his estates and dying in 1803. Lord Elcho was less fortunate. Owing, he believed, to the animosity of Cumberland, he was exempted from pardon and died in his old age in France, as did Lord Nairne. Lord Pitsligo, who had hidden with Nairne in Glenshee, preferred to skulk in Scotland; as also did Cluny, who spent nine years in his 'cage' on Ben Alder before going into exile. Lord Lewis Gordon died insane in France in 1756. A statement that he 'enjoyed no very sound health' during the campaign suggests that he suffered from mental trouble before Culloden, where there is no mention of his having been present.

After aiding the Prince in his wanderings, Lochiel escaped to France, where like Clanranald, Lochgarry, and others, he obtained a commission in the French army. He died of brain-fever in 1748. His brother, Archibald Cameron, executed in 1753, was the last man to die for the Stuarts. Ardshiel, after narrowly escaping capture in Appin, also found safety in France.

Sheridan died in Rome, heart-broken by King James's censure for his having encouraged the Prince to embark upon so wild an enterprise. Soon after returning to France, O'Sullivan was knighted, and later, on falling out of favour with Charles, secured his future by marrying a wealthy bride. He died, aged over 60, about 1761.

The Earl of Kilmarnock and Lord Balmerino suffered upon the scaffold, where old Balmerino's fine disregard of death evoked universal admiration. Although likewise found guilty, the Earl of Cromarty secured a pardon through the intercession of the Princess of Wales.

Sir John Cope died 'at an advanced age' in 1760, after peacetime service in Ireland. He is said to have made £10,000 by laying odds that his successor would be beaten by the Highlanders, just as he had been. Hawley, after further service in Flanders, was appointed Governor of Portsmouth. He died in 1759, aged about 80, and in his will (written by himself) expressed his hatred of priests and contempt for lawyers. Blakeney, still soldiering at 84, received an Irish peerage in recognition of his gallant, but unsuccessful defence of Minorca.

In some respects the subsequent lives of the two young commanders, whose armies had faced each other on Culloden Moor, resembled each other in the barrenness of their achievement. Unsustained by the faith that had supported his father in his many trials, and with no interests to fit him for private life, the Prince gave way to a fondness for wine, which had been noted with distress by King James before the '45, and with disgust by Elcho during the march to Derby. After his father's death he returned to Italy, but the 'King Charles the Third' who died at Rome in 1788 is more happily remembered as the 'Bonnie Prince Charlie' who captured Highland hearts.

The Duke of Cumberland's fighting career, which ended in 1757, was one of frustration and disappointment. Some words of praise for the dexterity with which he had handled a difficult retreat come, strangely enough, from Lord George Murray in a letter to his wife. Troubled by a leg wound received at Dettingen, the Duke was further incapacitated in his early forties by a stroke, asthma, and failing sight. His rough good-humour with his soldiers had been superseded by harshness, and he lost further popularity with them on account of his part in stiffening the Mutiny Act. He died at 44, but his name has lived on in Scotland as a symbol of brutality. Culloden was his only victory, but the price he paid for it, and for his ruthless harrying of the Highlands, was the unenviable title of 'The Butcher'.

From a medal commemorating
the battle of Culloden

Bibliography

MANUSCRIPT SOURCES

The Cumberland Papers — Royal Archives, Windsor Castle
The Blaikie Collection — National Library of Scotland, Edinburgh
State Papers 54–26 and 54–27 — burgh
The Forbes MSS. — Public Record Office, London
Unpublished letter and notes of Lord George Murray — Scottish Record Office, Edinburgh — Blair Castle
The Newcastle MSS. — University of Nottingham

PRINTED SOURCES

ATHOLL, John, 7th Duke of. *Chronicles of the Atholl and Tullibardine Families*. 1908.

BLAIKIE, W. B. (Editor). *Origins of the '45* (including 'Mr. John Daniel's Progress'. Scottish History Society, 1916.

—— *Itinerary of Prince Charles Edward Stuart* (including 'Lochgarry's Narrative'). Scottish History Society, 1897.

BROWNE, James. *A History of the Highlands and of the Highland Clans*. 2nd edition. 1845.

BURTON, J. H. *Lives of Simon Lord Lovat and Duncan Forbes of Culloden*. 1847.

—— (Editor). *Autobiography of . . . Dr. Alexander Carlyle*. New edition. 1910.

CADELL, General Sir Robert, K.C.B. *Sir John Cope and the Rebellion of 1745*. 1898.

CHAMBERS, Robert. *History of the Rebellion in Scotland in 1745, 1746*. 2 vols. New edition. 1828.

—— *History of the Rebellion of 1745–6*. 7th edition. 1869.

—— *Jacobite Memoirs of the Rebellion of 1745* (including Lord George Murray's 'Marches of the Highland Army'). 1834.

CHARTERIS, Hon. Evan. *William Augustus, Duke of Cumberland, His Early Life and Times*. 1913.

COPE, Sir John K.B. *The Report of the Proceedings and Opinion of the Board of General Officers on their Examination into the Conduct, Behaviour, and Proceedings of Lieutenant-General Sir John Cope, Knight of the Bath . . .* 1749.

Culloden Papers. 1815.

DICKSON, W. K. (Editor). *The Jacobite Attempt of 1719.* Scottish History Society, 1895.

DODDRIDGE, Dr. Philip. *Some Remarkable Passages in the Life of the Honourable Col. James Gardiner.* 1747.

DUKE, Winifred. *Lord George Murray and the Forty-five.* 1927.

DUNCAN, Captain Francis. *History of the Royal Regiment of Artillery.* Vol. I. 1872.

ELCHO, David, Lord. *A Short Account of the Affairs of Scotland.* Edited by the Hon. Evan Charteris. 1907.

FERGUSSON, Sir James, of Kilkerran. *Argyll in the Forty-five.* 1951.

FORTESCUE, Sir John W. *History of the British Army.* Vol. II. 1899.

GRAHAM, Dugald. *An Impartial History of the Rise, Progress and Extinction of the late Rebellion in Britain in the Years 1745 and 1746.* 1774.

GROSE, Francis. *Military Antiquities.* 2nd edition. 1800.

HENDERSON, Andrew. *The History of the Rebellion, 1745 and 1746.* 2nd edition. 1748.

—— *The Life of William Augustus, Duke of Cumberland.* 1766.

HEWINS, W. A. S. (Editor). *The Whitefoord Papers.* 1898.

HOME, John. *The History of the Rebellion in the Year 1745.* 1802.

HOWITT, William. *Visits to Remarkable Places.* 1840.

HUGHES, Michael. *A Plain Narrative or Journal of the late Rebellion.* 1746.

Jacobite Minstrelsy. 1829.

JOHNSTONE, Chevalier. *Memoirs of the Rebellion in Scotland in 1745 and 1746.* 2nd edition. 1821.

LEASK, J. C. and MCCANCE, H. M. *The Regimental Records of the Royal Scots* (including letter of Alexander Taylor). 1915.

MACGREGOR, A. G. Murray. *A Royalist Family and Prince Charles Edward.* 1904.

MCNEILL, P. *Prestonpans and Vicinity.* 1902.

MAHON, Lord. *The Forty-five.* 1851.

MARCHANT, John. *The History of the Present Rebellion.* 1746.

MAXWELL, James, of Kirkconnel. *Narrative of Charles Prince of Wales' Expedition to Scotland in the Year 1745.* Maitland Club, 1841.

METCALF, John. *Life of John Metcalf.* 1795.

MOUNSEY, George G. *Authentic Account of the Occupation of Carlisle in 1745.* 1846.

Memorials of John Murray of Broughton. Edited by R. Fitzroy Bell. Scottish History Society, 1898.

PATON, Henry (Editor). *The Lyon in Mourning.* Scottish History Society, 1895.

RAE, Peter. *The History of the late Rebellion.* 1718.

RAY, James. *A Compleat History of the Rebellion.* 1749.

RICHMOND, Admiral Sir Herbert W. *The Invasion of Britain.* 1941.

SALMOND, J. B. *Wade in Scotland.* New edition. 1938.

Scots Magazine. 1745 and 1746.

SINCLAIR, John, Master of. *Memoirs of the Insurrection in Scotland in 1715.* Roxburghe Club, 1858.

TAYLER, A. and H. *1745 and After* (including O'Sullivan's 'Narrative'). 1938.

—— *Jacobites of Aberdeenshire and Banffshire in the Forty-five.* 1928.

TAYLER, H. *A Jacobite Miscellany* (including part of Lord Elcho's ' Journal' and Sir John MacDonald's 'Memoirs'). Roxburghe Club, 1948.

TERRY, C. Sanford. *The Jacobites and the Union.* 1922.

—— *The Forty-five.* 1922.

The Trial of Archibald Stewart . . . for neglect of duty, etc. 1747.

TULLIBARDINE, The Marchioness of. *A Military History of Perthshire.* 1908.

VEZZOSI, Michele. *Young Juba: or, the History of the Young Chevalier.* 1748.

WILSON, Rev. William. *The House of Airlie.* 1924.

Index

The numerals in **heavy type** denote the figure numbers of the illustrations.

INDEX

INDEX

INDEX